A PLACE FOR LOST SOULS

Belinda Black is a Registered Mental Health Nurse, and a non-executive director of the Care Quality Commission (CQC), the independent regulator of health and social care in England. She began her nursing career in 1981, and over the following forty years worked in two large secure hospitals, a regional secure unit, as a court liaison officer at a secure unit for mentally disordered offenders, as the CEO of a Sheffield-based social care charity, and with the National Institute for Health and Social Care Excellence (NICE) to develop national guidelines for the delivery of health and social care. Belinda lives in Huddersfield. This is her first book.

A
PLACE
FOR
LOST
SOULS

A psychiatric nurse's stories of hope and despair

Belinda Black

with Rachel Murphy

QUERCUS

First published in Great Britain in 2023 by Quercus Editions Ltd
This paperback published in 2024 by

QUERCUS

Quercus Editions Ltd
Carmelite House
50 Victoria Embankment
London EC4Y 0DZ

An Hachette UK company

A CIP catalogue record for this book is available
from the British Library

PB ISBN 978 1 52942 968 8
Ebook ISBN 978 1 52942 966 4

10 9 8 7 6 5 4 3 2

Typeset by CC Book Production
Printed and bound in Great Britain by Clays Ltd, Elcograf S.p.A

MIX
Paper | Supporting
responsible forestry
FSC® C104740

Papers used by Quercus are from well-managed forests and other responsible sources.

To Jonathan, the wind beneath my wings.

CONTENTS

Author's historical note

From asylums to Care in the Community

I began my nursing career in one of the last of the UK's vast former psychiatric hospitals, predominantly working on its only locked ward, reserved for patients deemed in some way too dangerous to be cared for on the forty-plus 'open' wards. Though I didn't know it in the early 1980s, I was witnessing the end of an era in mental health care, one that had lasted for almost a century and saw thousands of patients with widely varying mental health diagnoses housed together – and in many cases becoming institutionalised – in huge, self-contained communities hidden away from mainstream society.

The Mental Treatment Act of 1930 overtook the Lunacy Act of 1890, renaming 'lunatics' as patients and asylums as mental hospitals. It was a landmark in mental health legislation and paved the way to the modern Mental Health Act, first introduced in England and Wales in 1959 and revised in 1983 and 2007. The legislation was and is designed to protect the rights of anyone with a mental health diagnosis who is made to stay in hospital for assessment and treatment.

Many of the patients I cared for on the unlocked long-stay wards had been admitted to the hospital prior to the introduction of the Mental Health Act 1959, and they simply never left. Several had arrived in the UK penniless and traumatised after the Second World War, survivors of concentration camps or prisoner-of-war camps. Plenty of patients had little command of the English language and no family to question why they stayed so long, or never came home at all. Too many of those who did have relatives had lost contact with them thanks to the old-fashioned system of discouraging visitors and restricting contact with family members, a policy that I'm sure contributed to the institutionalisation of so many patients who didn't want to leave the hospital even if they could.

The category 'moral imbecile' used to exist prior to the introduction of the Mental Health Act, which was defined in such vague terms that it allowed unmarried mothers to be detained in psychiatric institutions. I met at least one patient who fell into that category, while other patients had committed petty crimes that marked them out as 'wayward' or 'out-of-control' youths decades earlier. It's possible that in the mists of time they had been committed to the asylum on the recommendation of GPs or even local magistrates rather than psychiatrists, and in many cases the reason for their admission had been long forgotten.

The hospital I worked at was permanently shut down in the early 1990s when the government's policy of 'Care in the Community' brought the promise of more personalised patient care, either at home or in smaller units. The Community Care Act of 1990, which came into force in 1993, was the biggest change to mental health care in NHS history and by the end of the reform process more than 100,000 patients across the UK had been relocated.

I saw the hospital close down around me, the locked ward being the very last to shut. My final job there was to help my patients walk out of the gates, sometimes for the first time in decades.

Care in the Community remains the basis for community care as we know it today.

Confidentiality is key in nursing. While all the events described in my book are true, I have changed the names and other identifying characteristics of my patients, colleagues and the places I write about. Many of my patients from the old asylum have passed away, but as a sign of respect I have afforded them the same courtesy as those men and women who are still living amongst us.

Introduction

'I'm not going back to that place!'

'You bloody well are. I got you that job and no daughter of mine is going on the dole!'

My mother pulled back my duvet and dragged me out of my warm bed. It was 5 a.m. and I was due to work my second shift as a nursing assistant at the large psychiatric hospital on the outskirts of town.

'It's horrendous!' I wailed. 'No wonder everyone calls it the loony bin!'

My first day had been a baptism of fire, to say the least. I'd been put on a male rehabilitation ward for forty-five men of all ages, the vast majority admitted for their own safety, to stop them harming other people, or both.

As I protested loudly to my mother, unwelcome images of the day before were flashing through my head, frightening the life

1

out of me all over again. Most of the men were in the lounge area when I saw them for the first time, appearing like ghouls through a thick haze of smoke. They sat on plastic armchairs that were lined up around the edges of the dark, rectangular room, and every single one of them was puffing on a cigarette.

This 'day room', as it was known, was where the men from Ward 37 spent the majority of their waking hours, though it was the kind of place you wouldn't want to linger in for a moment longer than you had to. The windows were closed and the brown curtains drawn tight, trapping the most revolting smells inside. The stench of stale nicotine mixed with smelly bodies caught in my throat and made me want to retch, though I barely dared to breathe. I was rooted to the spot, squinting through the blue-grey fog at the weird, frightening-looking people I was expected to care for.

No. I can't do it! I'm not staying here!

No matter their age, or their shape or size, each man was dressed in the same hospital-issue uniform of a washed-out shirt and ill-fitting trousers, handed to them in 'bundles' from the store cupboard each morning. Some looked like they were chewing really hard on a toffee, or were trembling uncontrollably. Others were salivating and sitting strangely contorted in their chairs, looking dead-eyed or staring into a big plastic bucket full of cigarette ends, which stood on a square of dirty orange carpet in the middle of the room. I was so inexperienced I had no idea these were side effects of their anti-psychotic medications.

I looked around for signs of 'rehabilitation' but there were none.

There wasn't even a TV or radio in the room, just an old record player that stood dusty and silent in one corner. Nevertheless, an eerie soundtrack was swirling amidst the smoke. Some of the men were singing to themselves or throwing out random words and grunts while others were scratching or fidgeting noisily. Nobody was having a conversation, at least not with a person visible to the rest of us. The men didn't even look at each other. Sitting shoulder to shoulder, each patient appeared to be in a faraway world of his own.

I was just seventeen years old. As well as scaring the living daylights out of me, these were the saddest-looking people I had ever seen in my life. The hospital was everything I imagined a madhouse would look like. It felt like I'd walked into a remake of the film *One Flew Over the Cuckoo's Nest*, one that was being shot in a once-grand sixteenth-century family estate in the north of England.

My mother was a mental health nurse at the same hospital and had worked there for many years. 'You'll soon get used to it,' she was telling me as she ignored my protests and forced me to put on my shapeless sack-brown uniform, American-tan tights and sensible flat black brogues. 'Everybody does, you'll see!'

The hospital was one of the biggest employers in the area and lots of our friends and relatives worked there. It meant I already knew quite a lot about the place; it was impossible not to have soaked up at least some of its rich and colourful history. The original asylum had first opened its doors at the turn of the century and once treated 'shell-shocked' soldiers from the First World War, as well as 'pauper lunatics', a label from the Lunacy Act of 1890 that applied to anyone admitted to an asylum needing financial support.

These facts alarmed me when I first heard them. Black-and-white pictures of the old hospital had the same effect. Surrounded by vast acres of thick woodland, the main house looked like the sort of creepy place that would make a great location for a horror film. A clock tower rose above the imposing entrance, and I was fascinated to learn that once a week a maintenance man would climb the steps to wind up the clock with a giant key. I was also intrigued by the fact that up until the 1950s men and women were strictly segregated on the wards, as well as when they were allowed to dance or watch shows in the hospital's on-site ballroom.

The most violent and difficult-to-manage patients were kept in padded cells in years gone by, and the hospital had its own morgue and cemetery, where up until 1969 more than 2,800 patients were buried in unmarked graves, in many cases three deep.

Mum had once told me when I was younger that the trees in the grounds were tagged with different-coloured painted squares, so that patients who wandered off or were trying to escape could be relocated. I never forgot that story, and when I arrived on my first day I fully expected to see crazy, wide-eyed people clinging to the trees, waiting to be rescued, or being bundled into straitjackets. That didn't happen, though the tags on the trees were still there and, eerily, the decades-old system was still in use.

It was 1983 when I walked through the hospital's imposing gates for the first time, and by then it had expanded into an enormous, sprawling, self-contained community. As well as more than forty wards, it had its own pub, snooker room and tennis courts. The old ballroom was faded and creaking but still in use, while the archaic padded cells had been replaced with seclusion rooms containing a single mattress on the floor. There was also a small farm, allotments and greenhouses, and the hospital even had the luxury of its own water supply and a working fire station in the grounds.

Though I had no interest in becoming a nurse, I'd always been quietly intrigued by this unusual institution, wondering what really went on behind the red-brick walls of the historic old hospital. My mother often talked fondly of her job and of her patients, even the ones who had committed all kinds of crimes. She was never short of an amusing story to tell, either, though when it was my turn to work there, I couldn't imagine ever seeing the funny side. How could being shut inside in a loony bin all day be anything but grim, miserable and downright terrifying?

'Right, Belinda, get your coat on,' my mother was saying, the edge of her voice sharpening. 'We haven't got all day.'

My heart sank as I was unceremoniously shoved out of the front door, the refrain 'no daughter of mine is going to be a "one in ten"' ringing in my ears.

Britain was deep in recession. Margaret Thatcher was running the country, over two million people were unemployed and thousands more were joining the dole queue every day. It wasn't a good time to have left school with no qualifications, but I should have thought of that before. I'd preferred sneaking off to the corner shop to buy biscuits or having a crafty fag outside the school gates to sitting in the classroom, and now my chickens had come home to roost.

It was back to the madhouse for me.

The clang of the heavy door and the smell of disinfectant and stale smoke made my heart tighten in my chest. I was entering the male rehabilitation ward once again, and dread and doom were bearing down on me. As I pinned my plain white hat into my dark-brown hair I felt like a fraud and impostor. I should have been filled with compassion for the patients, but I felt only revulsion for the men I was meant to care for. A budding Florence Nightingale I most definitely was not. I would never make a good nursing assistant, I thought, let alone a mental health nurse, but what choice did I have? I just had to grit my teeth, roll up my sleeves and get on with it.

The memories I've just described are now decades old and I've since enjoyed an extremely rewarding forty-year career in mental health nursing, something I am so incredibly proud of. My first decade was spent in the same large hospital where I started as a nursing assistant, and where I was soon moved (with no say in the matter) to Ward 14, the hospital's notorious secure ward.

I completed my training as a registered mental health nurse and stayed at the hospital until its doors were shut for the last time in 1992, when 'Care in the Community' brought the closure of the last of the former asylums. I was forced to move on, along with patients who, in many cases, were terrified of leaving the only place they had ever called home.

It might surprise you to learn that after being so appalled about returning to the hospital at all, within a couple of months I'd completely fallen in love with my job. There was a particular day that allowed this to happen.

'Let's have some music on, shall we?' I said as I entered the day room of Ward 37 and greeted the patients with a cheery 'Good morning'. I'd become accustomed to the strange sounds and smells, and I was far less appalled by the appearance of the men on this rehabilitation ward. I smiled and said hello to them all, chattering away regardless of whether they wanted to join in a conversation.

'Shall we listen to "My Favourite Things"?'

I loved all the early 1980s music I listened to on the radio at home, or watched on *Top of the Pops*. Adam and the Ants, Dexys Midnight Runners, OMD, Madness, Roxy Music, UB40, I was into it all. There was a much more dated collection of music on offer on the ward, although after working my way through the old vinyls I'd become quite addicted to the soundtrack album from *The Sound of Music*. It was uplifting and joyful – just what I needed to help me through the day. I suggested we listen to it almost every day.

I lowered the needle onto the record and smiled to myself as Julie Andrews launched into the first line. I knew every word, and 'My Favourite Things' never failed to put a spring in my step. I wasn't ever sure what effect – if any – it had on the patients, because they generally just carried on smoking, chewing their imaginary toffees or staring into space. But today was different, because Olek, an elderly Ukrainian man, suddenly rose to his feet and started to sway. It took me completely by surprise. He always sat in the same corner and never said a word to anyone. I couldn't believe it, and then Olek walked over, took hold of me and started to spin me around the room.

'I'm glad you like this record, Olek,' I grinned. 'It's fantastic, isn't it?'

He could hardly speak any English, but his reaction was written all over his face: he was positively beaming. This frail, white-haired man had arrived in England at the end of the Second World War, having survived a Nazi concentration camp and all the horrors that entailed. I'd only ever seen Olek looking sad and dejected, and every day my heart went out to him as I found myself wondering what nightmares he'd lived through all those years ago.

Now his dazzling smile made him look like a completely different man. Holding my hand, he twirled me around the bucket of cigarette ends in the middle of the room, his eyes twinkling and a happy chuckle escaping from his lips.

It was a magical moment, one I'll never, ever forget. I could no longer see a tortured man who suffered with, amongst other things, paranoid delusions. Nor could I see the baggy hospital clothes that hung off his bent frame, or the strings of saliva on his stubbly chin.

'He's a person, just like me,' I thought.

It was such a simple observation, but it was also profound, and it's no exaggeration to say that moment changed my life. Olek, like all the other patients on this ward, was a human being. The men may have looked a little bit odd, they may have behaved in strange ways and had unusual thoughts, but they were the same as the rest of us, just a lot more misunderstood.

From that moment onwards I never looked back. My career had begun, and after that day I always looked forward to going to work. My enthusiasm never waned even when I was sent to work on secure Ward 14, letting myself in with a key every day and making sure the door was locked securely behind me, keeping the hospital's most dangerous patients safe inside.

It turned out I did have what it took to be a mental health nurse after all, and it's been a joy and a privilege to have worked with patients like Olek (and some very unlike Olek), for four fulfilling decades.

I'm writing this book for several reasons. I retired from nursing in 2021 (though I retain my registration, as I'm so proud to call myself a nurse), and this has given me a chance to look back on my long career. I realise I have a lot of stories to tell, ones that may make you laugh and cry as much as I did back in the day, and all over again as I've recalled them. Some might make your hair curl too.

More importantly, having witnessed the end of an era in mental health care, I think it's important to reflect on the mental health journey we've been on as a country. Nurses like me shoved keys in our pockets instead of tethering them securely to a belt, stony-faced sisters in starched white frilly hats patrolled the wards, and every patient was given milky tea with three sugars whether they liked it or not, ready-mixed in a gigantic teapot that served fifty cups. As the new girl, I would be tasked with swilling out the teapot before being dispatched to the hospital's own pub, where I'd ask the barman to fill the pot with lager for the staff to drink on the ward, a reward at the end of a shift.

Though only forty years ago, it was like another world compared to today. In telling the true, unfiltered story of this final decade of large-scale institutionalised mental health care, I hope to do my little bit for the history books, capturing moments that might otherwise be forgotten in time.

I also want to share some truths my career has highlighted along the way. A history of abuse – physical, sexual, psychological or a combination of the three – lay in the background of nearly every single patient I've ever nursed, not just in the 1980s but throughout my career. Though a very high percentage of my patients have committed crimes, the majority proved to be good people, or at least to have some good in them. I've found that most people do, if you take the time to look hard enough, and I count murderers and abusers in their number.

Looking back, it's hardly any wonder that I initially resisted working in the old 'loony bin'. Ever since the 1960s the media had been telling sad and shocking stories about the abuse and neglect of patients in asylums, and when the film adaptation of *One Flew Over the Cuckoo's Nest* came out in 1975 their image was tarnished further still, thanks to tyrannical Nurse Ratched's cruel mistreatment of the patients in her psychiatric hospital.

By the time I was a teenager the word 'asylum' had become synonymous with inhumane practices, human misery and long-term suffering, but unfairly so, in my experience. The word actually means refuge, protection, sanctuary and shelter, and I saw first-hand how, for many patients, the asylum system was very good indeed. During my time at the hospital the staff continued to refer to it as an asylum or a mental hospital, though both labels had been officially dropped by then. I still use the terms myself occasionally and make no apology, because I do so only with pride and not prejudice.

'Care in the Community' brought seismic changes to the structure of our mental health care system, though fundamentally not much has changed. People with mental health diagnoses are still detained against their will and locked up, sometimes unnecessarily, and for many years longer than they ought to be. They are simply put in smaller units now, ironically without the ready-made community the large, purpose-built asylums provided them with.

Ultimately, my experiences as a mental health nurse have taught me that we should judge less and open our hearts more. We are now in another new era, one in which mental health struggles are becoming ever more prevalent in our society. I hope my book will help reduce the stigma and increase understanding for anyone who is suffering with their mental health, and especially those whose diagnosis keeps them behind locked doors.

CHAPTER 1

'This stuff doesn't happen by magic'

Agatha and I burst into fits of laughter as we belted out the lyrics to Spandau Ballet's 'True', complete with our own exaggerated version of the chorus.

'Ha-ha-ha HAAA!' we chimed in unison as we bounded through the hospital grounds, arms interlinked.

Tonight was the night the local club put on a regular event for nurses, the 'event' being the lure of cut-price drinks to fill the venue on an otherwise quiet Monday. It worked like a charm. Hundreds of doctors and nursing staff would stream out of the hospital and head to Benny's nightclub in town, emerging in the early hours of the morning, blind drunk.

Another friend, Sally, had phoned me on the ward earlier in the day.

'I'm so pissed off I'm on nights,' she complained. 'Can you believe my luck?'

All the young nursing assistants looked forward to Monday nights. We'd finish our shift at 9.30 p.m., get the bus into town, drink in the Queen's Arms until closing time and then pile into Benny's until two or three in the morning. Afterwards we'd go to the Bombay Delight for a cheap curry to soak up the booze – in my case, pints of Holsten Pils with a double measure of Southern Comfort. If you were lucky you'd be on the 2–9.30 p.m. shift the next day, though we often started at 7 a.m., bleary-eyed and desperately lacking in sleep. Still, we just got on with it – only a night shift could spoil the fun.

'I'm going to have a couple in the pub at lunchtime to console myself,' Sally said, 'and then I'll get some sleep before I come in for my shift.'

A big part of my Monday night ritual was getting ready in the hospital with my friend Agatha. She was a couple of years older than me, but I was the one who owned half of Woolworths' beauty counter and I always did her make-up and styled her hair.

'What colour eyeshadow do you want tonight, Aggie?' I asked, setting out several palettes.

Agatha scoured them, a deadpan expression on her face.

'Blue?'

When I looked down I saw that every single eyeshadow was one shade of blue or another, and the same was true of my extensive collection of Cover Girl eyeliners.

'Blue it is, then!' I laughed. 'Great choice!'

We listened to a tape-recording of the Top Twenty as I did her eyes, singing along to hits like Heaven 17's 'Temptation', The Beat's 'Can't Get Used to Losing You' and New Edition's 'Candy Girl'. I'd not done a bad job of pressing play and record on my cassette recorder to cut out the DJ's chatter on Radio 1, and by the time I was putting the finishing touches to Agatha's hair, using mousse and rock-hard hairspray that turned it to rolls of black granite, we were belting out 'True' again at the top of our lungs.

Though none of the senior staff ever minded us getting ready to go out while we were still on shift, I always left it to the last minute to change out of my work uniform.

'Back in a minute,' I said to Agatha. 'My clothes are still in my locker.'

'No burries,' she breathed through the thick paper towel she was kissing in order to set her fuchsia-pink lipstick.

A long corridor with scratched Perspex windows ran the length of the narrow unit. The male and female dorms and individual bedrooms were at one end, a seclusion room, two lounges and the bathroom facilities in the middle, and the open-plan dining room was closest to the entrance at the other end. The nurses' office was about halfway along, and as I went to get my bag I was surprised to see Sally's silhouette behind the secure glass of the locked entrance door, grappling with her keys. Strange, I thought, given she was at least half an hour early for a shift she was very unwilling to do.

A moment later the door sprang open, clattering loudly into the wall and revealing a grinning, vacant-eyed Sally. My face fell.

She was balancing a pizza in one hand and waving an unlit fag in the other. Along with several patients and other members of staff I looked on aghast as she started to zigzag down the corridor, bouncing off the walls like a human pinball. When Sally reached the dining-room area she flopped into the nearest chair and tried to light her cigarette, though despite repeated attempts she failed to coordinate the flame with the fag.

'She's pissed,' screeched Victor, an elderly patient who arrived like clockwork every spring after suffering a manic episode. Victor was also a seasoned pub singer, and was in no doubt about what he was seeing.

Neil, the senior charge nurse (the male equivalent of a sister), looked at me in horror. 'Get her off the ward!' he yelled, raising his voice to an unusually high level. 'Now, Belinda!'

Neil had taken me under his wing when I started work on Ward 14. Of the more than forty psychiatric wards at the 3,000-bed hospital, this was the only secure one, its fifteen patients cared for behind a locked entrance door, as well as being shut inside their shared dorms or individual bedrooms at night.

The main function of Ward 14 was to offer treatment and care to high-risk, mentally disordered offenders whose law-breaking behaviour could include committing violent assault, arson or even murder. Some were on their way 'up' the system, having been sent from an open psychiatric unit, for example, while others were on their way 'down', having served time in a maximum security hospital like Rampton or Broadmoor. Whatever their crime, each was considered dangerous in some way, posing a serious risk to themselves, others and, in some cases, both. Alongside those men and women we also cared for patients who hadn't committed any offence but were violent, and those who the police had picked up on the streets and brought directly to us because they posed a potential threat (though in reality, they might have simply taken too many drugs). Suffice to say, the patients of Ward 14 were amongst the most vulnerable and dangerous in the mental health care system.

For practical reasons, we also took in patients who had run away from the other wards and simply needed to be locked up to stop them escaping again. It was common knowledge amongst staff that the phrase 'round the bend' was derived from the fact that the old asylums were purposely hidden away on the outskirts of towns, built at the end of long tree-lined driveways that bent at the end, so that the rest of society couldn't see the offending building or the 'lunatics' it housed. At least the old Edwardian prejudices served some purpose – our hospital fitted the picture very accurately, and absconders rarely got further than the hundreds of acres of woodland that shielded it from public view. Once escapees had been located, a group of strong nurses would be dispatched to restrain and reclaim them, using the rudimentary mapping system of trees tagged with different-coloured painted squares that my mother had told me about as a child.

Neil was a fair and equitable man and he'd instilled in me

the importance of being non-judgemental, whatever offences the patients had committed. I was there to provide care, he taught me, not to be 'judge, jury or executioner'. This was not a good situation for Sally to be in but I knew our senior charge nurse would treat her with the same kindness and compassion as he did all his patients, and this proved to be the case. In days to come there would be strong words rather than the threat of a disciplinary and Sally would sincerely apologise and promise never to repeat this mistake. First, though, she had to sober up, and out of sight of the patients.

Sally took quite a lot of persuading to leave the ward with me. Eventually I managed to steer her across the staff car park, where I made her sit in my burnt-orange Mini, the first car I got when I passed my test the year before, aged seventeen. 'Wait there until I finish my shift,' I said. 'I won't be long.'

'Righty-ho,' Sally slurred.

I left my keys, telling her to lock the door, stay safe and not move. 'Righty . . .' She was asleep before she finished her sentence.

Back in Agatha's room, I quickly changed.

'Is it new?' Agatha asked, admiring my outfit and smiling sweetly.

'Cheeky!' I said, checking the seams on my bright green ra-ra skirt, a perennial favourite I'd worn to death.

'You look great,' she said. 'Really good, Belinda.'

'You too. That lipstick really suits you. Right, then, time to go!'

I got to my feet, reminding Aggie I was leaving my box of

make-up, toothbrush and a hairdryer in her room, so we could do the same thing next week.

'Great!' she beamed.

A familiar mixture of sadness and wistfulness was welling up inside me as I walked towards the door. It was never easy leaving Agatha shut in her room while I went out dancing the night away, but I didn't ever let my feelings show. Getting ready with her was a ritual that had helped to bind us together, not just as patient and nurse, but as two young women who had become genuine friends. That, and leaving her with a smile on her face, was what I always tried to concentrate on.

Before my mother got me the job at the hospital I'd worked briefly as a carer in an 'old people's home', as we called them then, on one of Maggie Thatcher's Youth Opportunity Programmes. I was sixteen, and the senior carer, Ena, was an older lady who left a lasting impression on me. Her appearance alone was enough to do that – Ena had what you'd call a very hard face, coupled with dyed black hair that looked like it had been set in rollers her entire life. I tried to stay out of her way initially, though she turned out to be an incredibly kind person, one who taught me a great deal about how to make patients feel loved and cared for. She was particularly passionate about the importance of making someone feel completely comfortable and reassured at the end of the day, and she did this by giving her elderly residents a warm, bubbly bath and cuddling them dry with huge towels before tucking them into bed with a kiss on the forehead and a gentle hand on their arm.

Today's student nurses think that sounds daft or weird, not least because nowadays you aren't allowed to touch a patient unless it's absolutely essential to their care. But that old-fashioned sense of care and compassion was something that stayed with me throughout my career, and I always copied Ena's methods as far as I could. I'd like to think that Agatha felt the benefit of those old-school ways when I left her alone in her room, not tucked up in a cosy bed but inside a cloud of hairspray and love.

As I closed Agatha's door that night I saw Gayle, an experienced nurse, standing in the corridor outside. She was keeping a discreet lookout for me, which was something we did instinctively for each other all the time, whenever a member of staff was alone with a patient. I gave Gayle a thankful nod as she carried on her way, no doubt having to chase her tail even more now to get her jobs done.

A group of my friends went off to catch the bus, chattering away excitedly, while I walked back across the dark car park to deal with Sally. Like the vast majority of my colleagues, I never normally had any trouble switching into going-out mode when I left the hospital. It was vital to our well-being to do this, but tonight I found myself struggling, perhaps because I was on my own. Usually I would be with Sally. Also, I couldn't shake off the image of Agatha, shut up by herself in her room, with her hair and make-up all done and nothing to look forward to but her last shot of drugs to make her sleep through the night. And all while I went off dancing and drinking and having a great time.

Those patients who posed the greatest risk were generally the ones who had a bedroom of their own instead of sleeping on the single-sex dorms – either that or they were very long-term patients. I say bedroom, but in truth the individual rooms had more in common with a prison cell. Against my will I was picturing Aggie's single bed, bolted firmly to the floor, plenty long enough but barely wide enough to accommodate her short, spherical body. Next to the bed stood a dark-brown bedside cabinet, made of fake plastic wood, and on the wall opposite the door the small window had a bar across it, to prevent the safety glass from being kicked out. On the left-hand side of the room I could see the vandal-proof, murky plastic mirror above the sink, the kind you get in public toilets, and beyond it Aggie's wardrobe, also bolted to the floor. There were no pictures on the walls, no photographs on display. The only splash of colour was the hospital-issue, faded yellow quilt cover on Agatha's bed, and the bright red shoebox that held my cosmetics and hairdryer.

But all thoughts of Agatha disappeared when I found my Mini. It had been moved a few hundred yards down the road and Sally's head was hanging out of the driver's door, her long brown hair brushing the floor. She had obviously passed out again. I was used to this car giving me grief – it broke down all over town – but this was a dilemma I was wholly unprepared for, especially in stiletto heels that scratched across the tarmac as I struggled to shove Sally's dead-weight body across to the passenger seat. Still, I managed it, just about. It's surprising what you can do when you want to shake off the working day and get to the pub before last orders.

*

The first time I ever saw Agatha she was stalking down the corridor in the style of a younger, wider and squatter version of Miss Trunchbull, on the prowl for an offending child.

'Where is it?' she was yelling. 'Where's that baby? I'm gonna kill that fucking baby if she doesn't shut up.'

Christie, a nurse who'd worked with Agatha for years, was talking to her calmly, reassuring her that the baby's voice she could hear was nothing to worry about. It was coming from inside her head, that was all, and so she didn't need to go looking for a real baby, as there wasn't a baby on the ward. Did Agatha remember how they'd talked about that before, and how she mustn't get upset and angry like this?

'I'm gonna find it,' she bellowed. 'Where is it? Where's the fucking baby?'

Christie began steering Agatha gently but purposefully down the corridor, shadowed by a couple of nursing assistants who seemed to have been conjured from thin air, arriving on the scene like a pair of guardian angels. From a distance, I could hear the kerfuffle subsiding. Agatha had been given a dose of sedative before being settled into her bedroom, under observation.

'Good timing,' Christie said, her demeanour instantly changing as she checked her watch and scuttled back down the corridor towards the patients' dining room. It was 10 a.m., which meant it was time for the ten o'clock tray, when everything stopped and all the staff sat down with a tray of tea, milky coffee and hot, buttered toast. The same ritual took place at 6 p.m., and though

I was very new to the ward I already knew that nothing – and I mean nothing – disrupted this sacred routine.

Back on the long-stay wards where I'd worked, nursing assistants and domestics sat at one end of the room and the qualified nurses, sisters and charge nurses sat at the other. Everybody accepted this, not least because you'd have stuck out like a sore thumb, given that our pale-brown dresses might as well have been potato sacks compared to the dazzling white dresses worn by our superiors. We all wore white caps, but somehow the qualified nurses always managed to make theirs look brighter and whiter than ours.

In years to come I'd learn that the hierarchy was even more noticeable in general hospitals. My cohort of student mental health nurses looked shabby compared to the student general nurses, and we had to eat our food on the wards while the rest of the staff had their own dining area. The first dining room was a spit-and-sawdust kind of place with lino on the floor and long benches for the porters, domestics and auxiliaries to sit on; the next had proper chairs for the nurses and so on, the decor gradually improving in accordance with the rank of the staff. Last in line was the silver-service dining room, sealed off like a VIP enclosure for the exclusive use of consultants. Even back then, I was appalled by the division.

I'm happy to say that when I started work on Ward 14 everybody sat together, and the staff nurses were generally kind and welcoming to the young and unqualified nursing assistants like me. Team-building workshops and staff away-days had not yet been invented, but being locked inside together for long shifts (seven and a half hours at the start of my career, eventually rising to twelve), and at unsocial hours, helped forge strong relationships between staff. Meeting your partner at work was and still is something of an occupational hazard, and I was no exception to the rule. I married a nurse I met on the ward when I was a rather rash young woman, and after we separated I eventually settled down with my husband Jonathan, who I first met on our Registered Mental Nurse training course in 1986. Like many of us, Jonathan also had a strong family connection to the hospital, his mother having worked there for many years as a sister. Jonathan and I would go on to work hundreds of shifts together, and on one occasion we were one of four couples out of the ten staff on duty. We also knew plenty of colleagues who not only lived together but had previously been in a relationship with another nurse, just as I had. None of these relationships impeded patient care; if anything the opposite was true – the deep bonds we shared strengthened the nursing team as a whole.

Sharing a beer on the ward at the end of the shift was always a great way to connect with colleagues, even when you were the new girl who had to trek to the pub with the massive teapot. But it was the precious ritual of the tea tray that really bonded us, giving us such regular opportunities to chat and gossip, have a laugh and offer each other support, advice and a shoulder to cry on.

Shortly after I saw Agatha for the first time, patrolling the corridor and swearing angrily, I learned a great deal more about her over the ten o'clock tray – more than her bulging file of notes could ever have told me.

Diagnosed with paranoid schizophrenia, Agatha had been admitted to hospital five years earlier, at the age of fifteen. As well as hearing babies talking to her, the voices in her head called her names and insulted her, constantly telling her that she was fat, stupid and ugly, which sent her into violent frenzies. Agatha's mother – the only relative she was in contact with – believed her daughter was possessed by the Devil. 'She always brings in a big pair of red knickers when she visits her daughter,' one of the housekeepers said. 'She tells Agatha she must wear them to "keep the Devil away".'

As an uneducated teenager, I held the vague notion that schizophrenia meant having a split personality, half of the mind being invaded or controlled by the voices of the other personas who lurked within. In those days, the tabloid newspapers had a habit of referring to paranoid schizophrenics as 'schizos', and they fed the general consensus that those with the condition were unpredictable, dangerous and violent human beings. There is some truth in this – studies have shown that people with a diagnosis of schizophrenia are twice as likely to have a conviction for violence – but I was learning that the majority of sufferers are more of a danger to themselves than to others. In time I'd also come to understand that their problems are likely to have resulted from some sort of abuse or crisis they have suffered in their earlier life, the trauma perhaps provoking them to mentally escape to an alternative reality. It's thought the world that exists inside the mind of a person with schizophrenia offers a refuge, of sorts, from the infinitely worse terrors (or memories) that exist in the real world.

Kim, one of the more experienced nursing assistants, moved the conversation on.

'Agatha can be the funniest person,' she told me. 'Watch for the glint in her eye. She makes me howl with laughter sometimes, the things she does. But there's something you should know.'

I was all ears as Kim refilled her teacup, took a dramatic breath and began to recount her cautionary tale.

'I'm about to head home at the end of my shift when I hear a scream coming from Agatha's room,' she said, widening her eyes. 'And when I say a scream, I mean it was *blood-curdling*.'

The muted nods from the other members of staff confirmed this was no exaggeration.

'I've seen Sandy go into Agatha's room a few minutes before and so I turn round and start running back down the corridor. We're all running, even some of the patients are running. There's another scream and another, and then I hear a horrible clanking, banging sound.'

Kim paused and placed a protective hand on my sleeve before continuing.

'The voices in Agatha's head sometimes manifest themselves as the voices of nursing staff, you see. Agatha had grabbed Sandy by the head. Then she twisted her fingers through her hair real tight, and then she smashed her face into the radiator, not once but *repeatedly*. It took six staff to get Agatha off Sandy, but it would, wouldn't it?'

There was a chorus of 'Yeah, it would' around the table. 'She's so strong she once lifted two male nurses clean off the floor,' a male nursing assistant said, unable to disguise his admiration. 'They'd each taken hold of an arm as they tried to restrain her, but Agatha simply raised her arms out to the sides, the nurses still clinging on and with their feet swinging in mid-air, like a couple of cartoon characters.' Everyone laughed at this image, myself included; nobody had had to teach me that black humour is another very necessary tool in the psychiatric nurse's kitbag. 'Her arm was broken once, during a restraint,' someone else chipped in. 'I'm not being critical of anyone. Agatha's a seriously strong and violent woman, and for some reason she doesn't feel physical pain. Nobody realised what had happened until she said, "I think there's something wrong with my arm." It was flopping about all over the place, but she had felt no pain whatsoever.'

As soon as I saw a gap in the conversation I tentatively asked if Sandy was OK. Given that the radiators were made of thick columns of heavy metal, and it was in the days before protective covers were put over them, I think I already knew the answer. Heads began to shake despondently. Sandy, a pretty young woman in her mid-twenties, had suffered severe head and facial injuries. She was scarred for life and left the nursing profession soon afterwards.

*

Despite the fact I became good friends with Agatha, I knew there was a chance she might randomly attack me one day. It's not something I thought about on a daily basis. In the same way you can't allow yourself to dwell on the abject sadness of a patient's life, or take their problems home with you, you can't give in to fear or you wouldn't be able to do the job. When I looked at Agatha I invariably saw a young woman not much older than myself, one with a mischievous streak and the ability to crack me up laughing, just as she did the other nursing staff.

'Why do you keep looking at my tits?' she said to a wet-behind-the-ears junior doctor one day, completely out of the blue.

Her big brown eyes were fixed on his as she brazenly lifted up her T-shirt and flashed her large breasts at him. The doctor flushed bright red and didn't know where to put himself, shuffling off as quickly as he could without saying a word. I found it impossible to keep a straight face, and it was a story I enjoyed relating again and again in years to come, especially when one of my colleagues needed a laugh.

I was quite surprised that Agatha had the nous to pick on an easy victim for her prank, because when it came to understanding her illness she had no insight whatsoever. Nothing we said to her about the voices in her head being simply delusions got through. Some patients learn to live quite happily with their voices, accepting that they are ultimately harmless and can be ignored, if not turned off, but Agatha never could. The critical voices enraged her every time, and the baby who spoke to her almost every day was very real and always needed to be found, Agatha being convinced that the only way she could shut it up was by killing it.

Like many patients on the unit, Agatha was 'treatment resistant', meaning that the anti-psychotic drugs given to reduce or eliminate her paranoid delusions didn't have any impact on her symptoms. This was a problem for the doctors, whose principal role was to diagnose illness and prescribe medication. Given her unbending belief that the voices were real, the psychologists had a difficult job on their hands too, although one day a very superior and condescending female psychologist decided she knew precisely what to do.

'When you hear the voices in your head,' she said to Agatha, 'I want you to put in earplugs and jump up and down on the spot for five minutes.'

I think Agatha looked at her as disdainfully as I did, but still she did as she was told, bouncing off down the corridor like an out-of-control spacehopper, her fingers stuck firmly in her ears. Of course the laughable exercise didn't help Agatha one jot, as any member of the nursing staff who knew her well could have told the psychologist, had she deigned to ask our opinion.

I was sitting drinking a cup of coffee in the dining room one day, minding my own business, when Agatha came over without warning and walloped me on the side of the head. I'd probably spent hundreds of Monday nights getting ready in her room by this time and I'd known Aggie for many years.

What the—?

Before I knew what was happening she was wrapping her fingers really tightly into my thick head of hair, just as she had with Sandy. Luckily for me, several colleagues rushed in and instantly managed to restrain her, but she refused to let go, and her hand had to be cut out of my hair, leaving me with one side of my fringe longer than the other. Everyone knew I was a big fan of the Human League, so my colleagues were quick to point out that my lopsided hairdo bore no resemblance whatsoever to Phil Oakley's iconic, asymmetrical barnet, if that was the look I was going for. They were clearly trying to cheer me up. I managed to laugh, but afterwards I went to the nurses' office to phone Jonathan and found myself bursting into tears. It was unusual for me to break down but I'd never felt so shocked and betrayed. It all came flooding out when I heard Jonathan's voice. I'd been caring for Agatha for such a long time, I sobbed. She had never laid a finger on me and I hadn't seen this coming. 'Why now?' I cried. 'I consider her a friend. A very good friend.'

In fact, by this time I held Agatha in higher regard than some of my friends, and I spent more time with her than I did with my own family.

'I'm sorry, love,' Jonathan said. 'But you can't take anything that happens on the ward personally, you know that as well as I do.'

This was very true, but my usual optimistic outlook had deserted me. I couldn't help taking the attack personally, and I could hardly speak to Agatha afterwards.

It was about a week later, as I was still struggling to come to terms with what had happened, when Agatha came bowling up to me, tears dripping down her cheeks.

'I'm so sorry, Belinda,' she said. 'I'm really, really sorry.'

I'd just arrived for my shift and was very taken aback to see her like this. I hadn't expected this at all. I could see she meant it and was genuinely sorry, though given her lack of insight about her condition Agatha couldn't articulate what I knew to be true: that this was not an act of malice, but rather a response to voices in her head she was convinced she could not ignore.

'It's OK,' I said, giving her a hug. 'It's all forgotten now, we're friends.'

When I first met Agatha she was allowed to go home occasionally to visit her mother, but after one of these trips she returned to the ward looking sadder than I'd ever seen her. Eventually, Agatha explained what had happened. 'Mother took me to church,' she told me. 'The church members laid hands on me, to cast out the Devil that possesses me.' The home visits were stopped after that, though we couldn't prevent Agatha's mother from bringing in another pair of big red knickers every time she came to the unit. I didn't want Aggie exposed to any of that nonsense, and I'd always put them on the top shelf of the wardrobe, out of sight and where she couldn't reach them.

Whenever the doctors thought she was well enough Agatha was allowed to go out on accompanied visits into town, something I always enjoyed doing with her. It wasn't very long after the hair-grabbing incident when the doctors decided she was fit enough to go out on a shopping trip. I was delighted about this. Agatha loved these outings and was always happy to potter around the shops and sit in a cafe, drinking tea. Even just breathing different air was a treat, I imagined, and after what had happened between us I really welcomed the chance for us to spend a lovely afternoon together, outside the hospital walls.

Hilary, a colleague I'd worked with for many years, was the other nurse who came on the trip, as Agatha always had to have two members of the nursing team with her. Aggie was in her late twenties by this time and had spent nearly half her life locked on the ward, but if you'd seen us ambling around Marks & Spencer's that bright and sunny afternoon, you'd have taken us for three friends, happy in each other's company.

After we'd finished shopping we sat down in a popular cafe, glad to take the weight off our feet. Unfortunately, just as I was about to take my first sip of coffee I looked across the table and saw an unwelcome change in Agatha. After so many years of nursing her it was a look I was all too familiar with, and had seen many times before. The carefree expression she'd had on her face moments earlier had vanished, just as if someone had wiped it away with a big wet flannel. Instead the muscles in her jaw had tightened and her eyes were wide and expressionless as she began staring around the room, looking for the source of the voices that were taunting her. The fact that she had been doing well recently was irrelevant – this was exactly how Agatha looked when she grabbed my hair. I therefore knew *precisely* how this could end if we didn't intervene, and fast.

'Ring the hospital,' I said to Hilary, 'and tell them to come and get us, now!'

I had a bottle of anti-psychotic medication in my bag and I quickly poured some in a cup while Hilary phoned the unit.

'Here, Agatha,' I said calmly. 'Have a bit of this.'

She downed the liquid, but it was a desperate move given how resistant she was to medication. I could see that Agatha was deteriorating quickly, and as soon as she put the cup down she got to her feet, placed both hands under the wooden table and flung it up in the air with all her might. Given Agatha's strength, the small table nearly hit the roof of the cafe, sending cups of tea and coffee and custard slices flying everywhere. Gasps and shrieks rang out all around us.

'I'm gonna kill that fucking baby!' Agatha yelled, spinning round to face a horrified young mother whose child was lying in a pram next to her.

It was a very frightening moment. I felt genuinely afraid for the baby and could feel panic rising up inside me. The terrified mother shot to her feet, grabbed her baby from its pram and started to back away as fast as she could. Mercifully, there was a large table standing between us and the mother and baby, albeit one full of elderly ladies who also jumped to their feet, slopping tea and crying out in panic as they did so.

The mother made a frantic dash for the door, clutching her baby tightly to her chest. At the same time Hilary and I launched ourselves at Agatha, grabbing hold of her as tightly as we could

33

and somehow wrestling her heavy body to the ground. I don't know where our power came from, but somehow we managed it.

'I'm gonna kill that fucking baby!' Agatha continued to shout. 'Where is it? I'm gonna kill it!'

It sounded to me like the whole cafe was screaming now. Without saying a word to each other, Hilary and I quickly sat ourselves on top of Agatha, our combined weight just about enough to keep her pinned to the ground. This was not the way we'd been trained to restrain a patient, but in my experience it was very rare to carry out a textbook restraint. Averting disaster – and this could easily have been just that – was always uppermost in our minds. Besides, even if we'd had enough staff to do the job correctly, each taking an arm and making sure Agatha's head was properly protected, there wasn't enough space in this packed cafe to do it by the book.

'What the hell's goin' on?' I heard.

My heart was racing, adrenaline spiking through my whole body.

'What d'you two think you're doing?'

I looked round to see the flash of a yellow pinny. It belonged to the irate owner of the cafe, who was red in the face and brandishing a dripping mop.

'Help is on the way,' I said.

With the baby safely out of the way I was slowly starting to calm down, but the cafe owner was clearly extremely agitated and didn't seem to be listening to me.

'What the hell's going on?' she repeated. 'Get off her!'

With that she started whacking me and Hilary with the wet mop, bashing us on our backs and legs as she continued to screech, 'Get off her! Leave her alone!'

The penny finally dropped, bringing some welcome light relief. The cafe owner, who had obviously been in the kitchen and missed the drama about the baby, thought poor Agatha was being assaulted and she was only convinced otherwise when our uniformed colleagues arrived and carted Agatha off in an ambulance.

Agatha was never allowed to leave the hospital again after that, her care team deciding the risks were too great. It was a decision I reluctantly had to agree with. She could walk outside in the garden and take part in activities like art and cookery on the unit, but from now on there would be no shopping trips, no visits anywhere beyond the grounds of the hospital.

It wasn't long after this that Agatha was given clozapine, a powerful anti-psychotic drug used when all other medication fails. I was totally opposed to this, given that clozapine can have a flattening effect, stripping a patient of their personality and reducing them to a shuffling, salivating shadow of their former self.

'It will curb her violent tendencies,' the psychiatrist said, as if that were the only thing that mattered.

None of the senior professionals, including the doctors, occupational therapists and psychologists, knew Agatha like the nursing staff did. It was no fault of theirs. They never got the chance to wander round the gardens with their patients, do their hair or sing and play games together. The medics walked away and locked the door behind them after their routine visits and ward rounds. It was the nursing staff who were there around the clock, through the good times as well as the darkest and most intense ones.

Though mental health nurses don't prescribe drugs or give therapy like other professionals, we hold one of the most important keys to successful treatment. Building what's known as a 'therapeutic relationship' is vitally important to positive outcomes. It's our stock in trade, and it means carrying out a series of 'conscious actions', most of which come naturally to good nurses. The actions include showing the patient empathy and understanding, making it known you accept them without judgement, and demonstrating that you respect them and their beliefs, whatever they may be. Blow-drying a patient's hair, playing board games with them or having a cigarette together were therefore always more meaningful activities than they may have appeared. Once mutual trust and respect are in place, you are far better placed to understand your patient's needs and subsequently help improve the quality of their daily life and longer-term care.

I argued that the cost of prescribing clozapine was too great to a young woman like Agatha. She had already lost so much, why steal what little she had left of her life? My nursing colleagues supported me, but even as a collective we were arguing from a much weaker position of power. The psychiatrist's word was final.

It was heartbreaking to see our worst fears coming true as our lovely Aggie began to disappear before our eyes. The mischievous glint in her eye was extinguished, she started to dribble, was soon barely able to walk and became virtually mute. She also lost control of her bladder and put on stones of weight, making her morbidly obese.

Another side effect of clozapine is that it can lower the number of bacteria-attacking neutrophil cells in your blood, making you more susceptible to contracting serious, life-threatening infections. This happened to Agatha in time, something I was ultimately relieved about because it meant she had to be taken off the medication straight away. The potent drug needed time to leave her system, but I'm happy to say our Agatha gradually returned to us over the course of the next few weeks.

At the first opportunity I went with her into the grounds, linked my arm in hers and encouraged her to join in with a loud rendition of 'True', for old times' sake. It had been so long since we'd sung it I'd forgotten how poignant the words were. She'd 'come back again', thank goodness, but in Agatha's case that had to be enough. There would never be a ticket to the world, as the lyric went, not for Aggie. Persecuted daily by horrible voices, restrained by staff (and sometimes locked in seclusion), having medicines pumped into her and never enjoying the highs and lows of daily life like the rest of us: this was Agatha's life. No chance to go to university, no job, no celebrating life events with family and friends, never to be married or have children (the birth control pill was one of her daily medications), never to have her own home or to reach personal milestones. Agatha's life had been shrunk to fit inside the locked doors of Ward 14, where she was cared for by a succession of staff, some wonderful, some indifferent and some inadequate. It was rare for me to let so many sad thoughts fill my head, but this was the inescapable truth.

As well as forming a very tight therapeutic relationship with Agatha, I built up a particularly strong bond with three other patients on Ward 14 – Benedict, Rex and Jay.

'You smell,' I said to Benedict. 'Come on, in the bath!'

I would never normally speak to a patient like that, but I'd got to know Benedict very well and had learned it was the only way to get him to wash. He loudly refused to take a bath when any of the other nurses asked him to, and so it was always left to me to use a bit of cheek and charm to make him comply.

Benedict was in his fifties and, like Agatha, he was diagnosed with paranoid schizophrenia. He hadn't committed a criminal offence but was admitted because he was considered 'unmanageable', his main coping strategy being to shout and scream very loudly (and incomprehensibly). He would refuse to speak to anyone he didn't know, and when I first arrived on the ward he always looked the other way when I spoke to him, completely ignoring me. It took about a year before my offers to help him in any way were accepted, and then over various jigsaws, games of cards and copious mugs of tea in plastic cups, he gradually started to let me talk to him.

'Are you sure you want five sugars in your tea?' I'd gently tease, but only when I could sense he was in the right mood.

Despite the strong doses of anti-psychotic medication he was taking, Benedict had retained quite a lot of his naturally bright personality, and he usually enjoyed having a bit of banter.

'Yes, I do!' he'd grin. 'And what are you going to do about it, Belinda? Will you call the sugar police?'

Despite the giant teapot being routinely loaded with approximately three sugars per cup of tea, Benedict always wanted more, and he would help himself to the sugar pot, loading two more rounded teaspoons into his mug, at least. He was one of the unhealthiest people I knew, constantly chain-smoking and eating sweets and biscuits. As a long-stay patient you received a small amount of money every week from the government. This was written on a card which the patient took to the hospital shop, the amount they spent being deducted and their balance marked on the card. A member of staff would have to accompany the patients of Ward 14 to the shop on the other side of the hospital, or a nurse went to the shop for them if they weren't able to do it themselves. However, it was up to the patients what they spent their money on, and there was nothing we could do if someone wanted to spend every penny on junk food, cigarettes or sweets and sugar-laden treats as Benedict did.

I'd just roll my eyes playfully when he sat there puffing on his hand-rolled cigarettes, eating Spangles and custard creams and drinking his calorific tea. My job was to connect with him, not lecture him about his lifestyle, although eventually we did try to teach him how to cook, which improved his diet fractionally, I think.

One day Benedict refused to take his tablets. 'I don't like the colour yellow,' he told me. 'I'm not having them.' He wasn't joking. He wanted green tablets instead of yellow, and he wasn't shifting.

I'd never been so pleased to see that it was Dr Yorke on duty that day. He was a really good, caring man who accepted unquestioningly that this was important to Benedict, immediately making it his business to source green tablets that did exactly the same job as the yellow ones. I knew plenty of other consultants who would have refused to engage with such a request, but Dr Yorke understood what this meant, not just to Benedict, but to all the nurses like me who had to dish out his medication and needed to maintain the best possible relationship with our patient.

Unfortunately, shortly after this incident, a newly arrived student nurse was not as adept at reading the room as Dr Yorke, and she was about to learn a lesson she would never forget about patient/nurse relationships. Having seen me in action with Benedict, the next time he was overdue a bath, stinking out the corridor as he often did, she walked boldly up to him, put her hands on her hips and told him loudly, 'You smell!'

Benedict stopped in his tracks, swung round and punched the poor girl straight in the face. I felt very sorry for her, but at least she would never make this kind of mistake again.

Rex was a large, squat man with a wiry beard who loved soul music and had a voice deeper than his idol, Barry White. He was in his early thirties when I first met him, and remained on Ward 14 throughout my time there. Very unusually, Rex's loving family was extremely involved in his care.

Historically, asylum patients were taken away and rarely returned to families, those in charge believing it was best to sever all contact. Relatives were very often relieved because it took away the shame of having someone with mental ill-health visible in their family. When I first started work on the long-stay wards at the hospital, visiting was only allowed on Saturday afternoon between two and four. It wasn't until the mid-1980s that the importance of family and maintaining family connections even started to be thought about, never mind acted upon. Nevertheless, though wards now have open visiting hours, many mental health patients still don't have visitors. On the last ward I worked on in 2021, for instance, of twenty patients only three or four had any form of regular contact with their family.

This was not the case with Rex. He had a twin sister he was particularly close to, and the family used to take him out and have him home for the weekend as often as he was allowed. During one of these visits he smashed out every window in the house, but even after that the family still insisted on having him to stay as often as the doctors would permit. In the aftermath of his wrecking spree Rex was mortified about the damage he'd caused. Unlike many other patients, he had a great deal of insight into his mental health condition and was quite tortured by his feelings of remorse. He also felt generally inadequate for being locked inside a hospital.

'Their lives are going on without me,' he said to me one day, shaking his head.

I admit it had taken me a while to warm to Rex. He had a history of being 'too familiar' with little girls, which I found extremely difficult not to judge. He had also once carried out a calculated attack on another member of staff, lying in wait behind a door, smashing an ashtray into his face and attempting to gouge out one of his eyes.

Despite Rex's flaws and failings I gradually started to get to know the good person inside. The psychiatrists supplied the same pills to him whatever mood he was in, governed by the need to reduce his risk of violence. But the nurses who spent hours on end with him got the chance to see Rex as a real, multilayered person. On lucid days he was kind, thoughtful and considerate, asking after patients who'd had a bad night, politely letting others be served from the food trolley before him and waiting patiently for help if he could see we were run off our feet. It was nursing Rex that really brought home to me that most people have some good in them when you properly get to know them, and when you look hard enough.

Unfortunately, when it came to Jonathan, Rex could see no good at all. He hated his guts and never held back in saying so.

'I fucking hate Jonathan Black,' he would shout out randomly, all over the ward and at the top of his voice. 'I fucking hate Jonathan Black!'

Jonathan was slim and very good-looking, and I assume Rex

was jealous of him. Neither of us let the taunts bother us. We both knew the sides of Rex that weren't nice were the result of illness, not badness.

Jay was carried onto the ward one Saturday morning as if he were a long, awkward parcel. The police had 'subdued' him, they said (I'm not sure how) after he smashed his luxury sports car into several police cars that had surrounded him in the street. The officers had been called out by terrified members of the public who had seen Jay standing in the middle of the road with his samurai sword, striking a series of menacing poses. He was dressed as he always was, in a black T-shirt, leather trousers, a long black leather coat and his prized Indian Kufi-style cap, and when the first officers arrived he completely ignored them and carried on wielding his sword before jumping back into his car and crashing into the police vehicles. Given that Jay was over six feet tall, he made quite an intimidating sight if you didn't know him – and sometimes if you did.

'OK, take the handcuffs off,' I said to the officers, 'and put him down.'

I knew that Jay was a naturally sweet and kind young man. He was in his mid-twenties and came to us two or three times a year when his paranoia exploded into violence, typically targeted at the police. Jay had taken a lot of Class A drugs in his time and when he wasn't admitted to the ward he lived a privileged lifestyle involving more cocaine, nightclubs and girls. All of this was funded by his very wealthy, glamorous mother who would do anything for her only son. Jay's father, meanwhile, was an aggressive man who ran a chain of nightclubs and was something of a Mr Big in the town. He thought Jay's mother had made him 'soft' and turned him into a 'wimp'. He also refused to accept that his son had mental health problems of any kind, and consequently he never visited him in hospital.

The police were reluctant and very worried about releasing Jay from their grip, but given how frequently he was admitted to the ward, I and the other nurses on duty knew how to handle him. We'd built up a strong relationship with Jay over the years and we knew he always responded well to us, no matter what his mental state.

'He'll be fine,' I said. 'Take the handcuffs off, please. And where is his hat?'

Jay was a very attractive young man but he suffered from premature baldness and we knew it was extremely important to him to hide this under his cap. The officers didn't have an answer and I wondered if they'd deliberately left the cap behind to punish Jay. Whatever had happened to it, I knew Jay had an extensive collection of weird and wonderful hats and I assured him I'd get his mum to bring another one in soon.

'Don't worry,' I said, marching him swiftly down the corridor and settling him in a single bedroom. 'I'm sure she won't be long.'

When Jay emerged after his mother's prompt visit he had a beautiful black and gold cap on his head and looked like a weight had been lifted from his shoulders. Over a cigarette later he told me how he'd repeatedly shunted back and forth between the first two police cars that blocked him in, then deliberately smashed into the three other vehicles that arrived with sirens blaring.

'Belinda,' he said, laughing. 'I saw all the squad cars and vans. I thought "fuck it" and smashed into them as fast as I could.'

A few days later I was very fed up to discover there were only three staff on duty instead of the usual six or eight. We couldn't get any more staff so we'd just have to get through the day as best we could. The ward was particularly disturbed at that time, a higher than usual number of patients having been brought in by the police like Jay, the only difference being that most of them were actually dangerous.

I was the nurse in charge tonight, the other two members of staff being young and inexperienced support workers.

'We could be in for a bumpy ride here,' I said.

I needn't have worried. To my surprise, the shift turned out to be one of the quietest I could recall, all the patients being as good as gold, and some going out of their way to make my job easier.

I discovered later that when Jay got wind of my predicament, he had gone round the whole ward in his full black-leather warrior outfit, flexing his muscles and warning every single patient to behave themselves, or else. I always felt his choice of clothes was his protection against the world, but on this occasion he used it to protect me and my colleagues, something I was very touched by.

'You deserve it,' Jonathan said. 'This stuff doesn't happen by magic.'

Thinking about the years I'd spent not just nursing but getting to know my 'family' of patients, including Agatha, Benedict and Rex, I was proud to take the compliment.

CHAPTER 2

'You have to be an optimist to do this job'

'I'm going to cut the patients' hair,' Sister Kane said, giving me her trademark sunny smile.

'Oh, right, Sister,' I replied, trying to stop my jaw from hitting the floor as I looked at the brown ceramic pudding bowl and large pair of gleaming scissors in her hands.

I might have been a very wet-behind-the-ears nursing assistant – I was just a few months into the job and still finding my feet on the unlocked wards – but even I knew that setting up a makeshift hairdresser's couldn't be normal practice.

I liked Sister Kane a lot. She was in charge of a women's ward for long-term patients, most of whom were middle-aged or elderly and clearly loved and respected Sister Kane. Christmas was coming, and the long-running tradition was for each ward to set up its own little drinks cabinet so nurses could visit each other's wards to toast the season. Sister Kane was bright and jolly at the best of times, and today she'd been exuding even more warmth and enthusiasm than usual. The Babychams and snowballs might have had something to do with it – we'd all had a couple of tipples by lunchtime, and there was a terrific buzz in the air. Or at least there was until the moment Sister Kane emerged from the kitchen with the pudding bowl and scissors.

My heart was in my mouth now, and I was watching with bated breath as Sister Kane pulled out a chair and beckoned over her first 'client'.

'Come on, Linda,' she said, flashing a radiant smile as she ushered a large woman with thick, shoulder-length grey hair towards the black plastic chair. As with most of the women on this ward, when I asked an older colleague why Linda was there I was simply told, 'She's been here for years, love,' as if that were a diagnosis in itself.

'Come and sit here, my lovely,' Sister Kane said kindly.

Oh my God! No!

Linda dutifully did as she was told, smiling as Sister Kane placed a stiff, grey-white hospital towel across her shoulders.

I'd learned so much about good nursing practice from seeing Sister Kane at work. Round and squat, she looked like a kindly aunt, one who was bursting at the seams with goodness and generosity. She never failed to give you a beautiful smile, and she was by far the most tactile of all the nurses I'd come across, always putting her arms around the patients and giving them a proper, good cuddle. But what I admired most of all was that Sister Kane always made time to talk to her patients, no matter how busy or tired she was, or how long it was past the end of her shift.

Not surprisingly, her relationship with her patients was incredibly strong. I could see that the women trusted Sister Kane and felt safe in her hands, because they knew she genuinely cared about them. 'And whatever you might think, the patients *do* know which nurses care and which ones couldn't care less,' Sister Kane had cautioned me when I first arrived on her ward. In years to come, and as the rules and regulations became more oppressive, I never forgot that. As I mentioned before, in today's hospitals you can't touch patients unless it's absolutely essential. This means that sometimes the only time a patient has any human contact is when they are being restrained, which saddens me. However, 'Actions speak louder than words,' was another lesson Sister Kane taught me. I might not have been able to cuddle a patient, or even touch the back of their hand to offer some comfort, but I could always smile and give my time generously – there have never been restrictions placed on that.

'Here we go, it won't take a minute!'

I watched with mounting panic as Sister Kane planted the upturned bowl on Linda's head and proceeded to chop off every piece of hair that stuck out from under its rim. Like nearly all of the patients on this ward, Linda had been locked inside the hospital for so long she had become completely institutionalised. She sat humming quietly to herself as chunk after chunk of her thick hair fell to the floor, and when the bowl was lifted off her head she simply stood up and shuffled away as if nothing had happened.

It was Valerie's turn next. The fact that Linda looked like she'd cut her own hair, in the dark and with a pair of garden shears, didn't appear to put Valerie off at all. Just like Linda, she trusted Sister Kane implicitly, sitting perfectly still as the bowl was lowered onto her head and the rapid snip-snip-snipping began in earnest once again.

Sister Kane was racing through the haircuts at a rate of knots. Most of the patients had looked strange in some way to begin with, but now they were starting to resemble a ragged assortment of scarecrows. Poor Valerie's fringe was hacked off at an angle and sat like a crooked cap across her forehead, and another patient had such a short haircut that her large ears were exposed like two teacup handles. I didn't know whether to laugh or cry, though all the patients remained unperturbed.

'Oh, Sister Kane, do you think you should be doing that?' I mumbled, eventually. It had taken me far too long to pluck up the courage to say something, but when you're the new girl in the brown sack dress you don't challenge the matriarch in the smart navy-blue uniform and pristine frilly white hat.

'Next!' Sister Kane called, completely ignoring me as Olive, a woman with two long thin plaits, settled in the chair.

No, not the plaits! The plaits looked older than me, I thought. Olive must have had them since at least the 1960s. *This has got to stop!*

'Merry Christmas!'

I swung round to see two nurses bursting through the double

doors to our ward. They'd come to have a drink with Sister Kane, but as soon as they saw what she was up to the smiles left their faces. Sister Kane's pop-up hair salon was swiftly shut down and she was gently but firmly steered off the ward. Thankfully, Olive's plaits were spared.

Despite being such a newbie I'd already witnessed quite a lot of surprising and unconventional practices at this hospital, and I didn't think for one minute that this would signal the end of Sister Kane's career, but sadly it did. She was subsequently removed from her post, and I never saw her again. Almost ten years later, when the hospital was about to shut down, I was in the staffroom when I heard two old colleagues chatting.

'Did you hear about Sister Kane?'

My ears pricked up, an image of Sister Kane's smiling face appearing in my mind's eye.

'No, what?' the other nurse said.

'She's dead.'

'No! How?'

'Killed herself, poor love.'

My heart fell to my feet as I listened to the rest of the conversation, too stunned to join in.

'No! That's awful. Mind you, she did have her problems, didn't she?'

Sister Kane would have been in her fifties, I heard someone else say. She had never married or had children, and she'd died alone at home, having taken an overdose.

My brain was scuttling back in time now. I'd learned a lot about Sister Kane after she was dismissed. She had bipolar disorder, known then as manic depression, although as an inexperienced seventeen-year-old I understood very little about it.

Sometimes Sister Kane sat alone in her office for her entire shift, not wanting to talk to anybody. On other days she experienced the other extreme – the 'high' end of her disorder. She would laugh longer and louder than everybody else when a joke was told, she would squeeze you a bit too tightly when she gave you a hug, and she could behave in an inappropriate manner with the patients, as I'd seen for myself. The hair-cutting debacle was the final straw for the hospital managers who, I would later learn, had tried for many years to accommodate the challenges of Sister Kane's condition.

Sister Kane's career had been littered with mental health incidents, including one time when she was found dragging a sack down the middle of the runway of the local airport. As a result, she was sectioned, brought into the hospital and placed on a neighbouring ward to the one she was in charge of, where she was looked after by nurses who knew her personally. When she was better she returned to work as a sister, with all and sundry knowing her business, including the fact that she was taking lithium, the drug of choice then for patients with bipolar disorder. Used to stabilise the mood so that the patient suffers less extreme highs or lows, lithium has been quite successful over the years and still is, although it can take away a bit of your personality too, the crashing lows and manic highs replaced with a steady flatness.

That's one reason some patients simply decide to stop taking it, sometimes with the most tragic consequences.

These days, Sister Kane would be moved out of the area to be treated and, if she were allowed to come back to work, she would most likely return as a staff nurse with a proper support plan, rather than resuming her job as a sister. Had the latter happened, Sister Kane's career, and quite possibly her life, might have been saved.

Suicide used to be a taboo word inside mental hospitals. We were discouraged from talking about it in the 1980s, for fear it might 'put ideas' in a patient's head, leading them to thoughts they might not otherwise have had. Now we positively encourage patients to talk about their suicidal thoughts and we carry out detailed assessments to help predict suicidal behaviour and intention, in order to rate a patient's risk of taking their own life. 'What do you think you will be doing next week?' is a typical question. Some people give you a surprisingly positive answer, talking about a date in the diary or a meeting they will attend, even though they've just told you they are desperate to kill themselves. Others will reply: 'Next week? I don't see a future. I can't think about it. There's nothing there.'

Assessments like this help us give patients the best possible care plan, usually combining medication with talking therapies. It's a massive improvement on the wall of silence and doses of lithium we used to offer up, and thankfully we have seen a decrease in suicides. In 1981, the Office for National Statistics recorded the suicide rate as 14.7 deaths per 100,000 in England. By 2021 this figure had fallen to 10.4 deaths, although suicide remains the biggest killer of men under forty-five. Clearly, we are still not doing, or talking, enough.

Four particular patients always come to mind when I think about suicide, their stories having given me an insight into the darkest corners of human suffering.

When I was ushered into the home of Alfred's brother, I winced. *What are the chances? This is the last thing we need.*

Alfred's brother Wesley was having a party, and his living room was packed with people who were not yet drunk but, let's say, 'fresh'.

'Come on in, love,' Wesley was saying. 'Don't be shy. What did you say your name was, again?'

'My name's Belinda,' I repeated, louder this time, as I was competing with Whitney Houston's 'I Wanna Dance With Somebody', playing at high volume on Wesley's stereo.

'Like I say, it's about your brother, Alfred. Can I talk to you privately?'

'It's OK, love,' he said, smiling and looking around at the packed room. 'Whatever you've got to say, you can say it in front of all these good people.'

It was soon after the closure of the asylum and I was working as an operations manager in a smaller secure unit. I'd been working at home, on call, when I learned that Alfred, a ninety-three-year-old man, had killed himself. He'd done this by throwing himself over the banister of the stairs on the third floor of the hospital, where he had a clear fall through the middle of the wide, spiralling staircase to the ground floor. He'd died instantly, his body landing on the hard black-and-white tiles that covered the unit's ground-floor reception area.

I didn't know Alfred personally, but the member of staff who informed me of his death told me he was a lovely old boy who was 'just tired of living'. His wife had died many years before and his brother Wesley, who I reckoned to be in his early seventies, was his only surviving relative.

A very shy junior doctor had accompanied me to Wesley's end-of-terrace house to deliver the bad news, but he was about as much use as a chocolate fireman, hovering two paces behind me with his lips buttoned shut.

'Really, I'd like to talk to you in private,' I repeated, but Wesley was adamant it wasn't necessary, telling me all over again that whatever I had to say, I could say it in front of 'all these good people'.

Someone was lowering the volume on the stereo and people were turning to look at us. I glanced over my shoulder to see the junior doctor looking as mortified as I felt. He also seemed to be incredibly interested in the stitching of his black leather brogues.

I had no choice, and so I cleared my throat, took a deep breath and told Wesley that his brother had passed away earlier that day.

The news brought the room to a standstill. Whitney Houston was still singing in the background but everybody suddenly stopped talking and stared at us. It was like that scene in a film

55

where the needle on the record scratches off and an awkward silence descends on the room.

'Right,' Wesley said, reaching for a cigarette. 'You'd better come into the kitchen, love.'

A death like Alfred's would not happen today. We are far more clued-up about suicide risks and health and safety in general, and open spaces beneath flights of stairs are blocked in, making it impossible for anyone to fall between several floors, deliberately or otherwise.

Alfred's death could have been avoided, but was it so terrible that he took control of his own fate? He was a very old man at the end of his life, he'd had enough of living, and death was what he craved and wanted. Alfred had got his wish.

I've encountered a small number of patients who are so unhappy and have such a miserable existence that they also do not want to be here any more, and this feeling does not pass over time.

I didn't know Shirley very well, but I looked after her for a short time and I knew something of her history, which was heart-breaking. A small, meek-looking woman in her forties, Shirley had been feeling suicidal ever since her two young children had died of cancer many years earlier. Her husband subsequently abandoned her to a psychiatric hospital.

Had suicide assessments been in use in the early 1980s, Shirley would have been the highest-scoring patient I ever met. Her risk of suicide was off the scale. Not only could she see no future, but she didn't want to see one. Such was the suffering she had endured, and for so many years, that she simply didn't want to live any more. She was actively suicidal, and by that I mean she was constantly thinking of how she could kill herself. This was not a 'cry for help' in any way, as Shirley genuinely, and desperately, wanted to end her time on earth.

Patients intent on killing themselves can be very resourceful. Back then patients used uncovered radiator pipes, taps, light fittings, you name it, as ligature points. We had a lot to learn, and nowadays furniture and curtain rails are collapsible so they can't withstand body weight.

Shirley was under the highest level of observation, at all times of the day and night. If she had been allowed outside, she told me, she would have thrown herself under a bus or jumped off a bridge. I didn't doubt that for one moment, and neither did the psychiatrists who were ultimately in charge of patient care.

'I am so, so miserable,' Shirley said to me, over and over again. 'Please can I just die? What is the point in keeping me here like this? It's no life. I have no responsibilities to anyone. My husband doesn't want to know me. I don't want to be alive. Please let me go!'

The first time she said this I remembered my mother telling me about something called a 'Brompton cocktail'. Nurses on the psycho-geriatric ward, as it was known in the 1960s and 1970s, would administer this concoction of alcohol, morphine and cocaine to patients who were ready to die, wanted to die and, crucially, were in pain. The morphine suppresses breathing and eventually shuts down the respiratory system, leading to death, and the nurses were not afraid to use it – and were trusted to do so – where they saw fit. Overwhelmingly, it was viewed as a compassionate act, and the nurses were allowed to get on with it, in the same way specialist nurses are trusted to administer increasing doses of morphine to dying cancer patients today.

Now, thanks in no small way to the 'Shipman effect' – changes made to medical practices after the conviction of the serial-killer GP Harold Shipman – we are so risk-averse that when, for example, a ninety-year-old patient with no quality of life contracts an infection, he or she is rapidly transferred from the mental health unit to a general hospital and given IV antibiotics. Anything less might be interpreted as medics 'playing God' as Shipman had done, and that risk simply cannot be taken. I understand this. Above all else, our duty is to protect our patients. But have we really made progress in cases where treatment is administered rapidly to patients who are no longer capable of articulating their wishes, or whose own views are overruled?

None of the drugs Shirley was given made any difference to her, which didn't surprise me at all. In the months I nursed her I saw no evidence that she might have a mental health disorder, and she was not diagnosed as being clinically depressed. In my opinion – and I was not alone in this view – she was suffering from acute unhappiness. Understandably, she wanted her unhappiness to end.

It was many years later when I heard that Shirley had finally got her wish by hanging herself. I was sad to hear it, but I felt relief that her suffering was over.

When I reflected on her passing in later years, I wished Shirley had been allowed a peaceful and dignified death, and one that was as pain-free as possible. If you haven't got a mental health condition and no drugs are helping you feel better, I believe you should now be able to choose to die in the same way a terminally ill patient has the right to travel to Switzerland and end their physical suffering at a Dignitas clinic.

The suicide of Christine in the first half of the 1990s has also stayed with me. It happened when I was working for a small secure unit after the closure of the large psychiatric hospital, and when I went to inform her mother and grandmother of her death I was with the same apprehensive doctor who'd accompanied me to Wesley's home. This time, instead of hovering a few paces behind me, the junior doctor pushed me forward as the front door opened.

'You don't need to tell me,' Christine's wild-eyed mother screamed. 'You've killed her, haven't you?'

Before I could say a word in response the door was slammed in our faces, Christine's grandmother shouting abuse at us from the hallway. Whatever you thought of these two women – and all of the staff on the unit had something to say about them – they had good reason to be as angry as hell.

'It should be you telling them, not me,' I thought, turning to look at the ashen-faced young doctor recoiling behind me. Although, to be fair, wherever you stood in the professional pecking order, nobody got paid enough to deliver news as desperate as this.

In recent weeks Christine's mother and grandmother had been stopped from visiting her, which was something they had done as frequently as possible from the day she was admitted, always staying for hours on end. There were various reasons the decision was taken to keep them away. Christine's mother had a habit of sitting the very petite young woman on her knee, rocking her like a baby and cooing over her. Meanwhile, Granny would stroke Christine's mousy brown hair, or what was left of it, given that the poor girl had alopecia and her unusually large head was covered in several smooth and shiny bald patches. We suspected there was a history of abuse in this dysfunctional family unit, but it was impossible for Christine to be properly assessed while her relatives were smothering her like this. They were also rude and aggressive towards the staff and they kept interfering with Christine's care plan, complaining incessantly about the drugs she was prescribed and the treatment she was given.

'Don't talk to 'em,' her mother had been overheard saying one day.

Christine did everything her mother told her and wouldn't communicate with us at all after that, and she also mimicked her mother's rudeness, verbally abusing the staff and behaving aggressively towards us. After attempts to limit their visits didn't work, the hospital administrator felt he had no choice but to ban the two women from coming onto the ward at all, a decision that sent them into a furious rage.

'It's for Christine's benefit,' they were told. This was true; in order to give her the best care, we needed to get a proper, uninterrupted view of this young woman. 'She is in good hands,' the relatives were assured, 'and we want the very best outcome for Christine, just as you do.'

I had had a battle putting those words out of my head as I'd headed to the family home with the doctor. Christine was a high suicide risk and had been placed on fifteen-minute observations throughout the night, yet despite this she had still managed to strangle herself, using a piece of her clothing as she hid beneath her bedcovers. The nurses who observed her assumed she was fast asleep under her quilt when they looked through the viewing window in her door, ticking off each 'observation' on the chart as having been completed. Except the observations hadn't been completed at all, because what they should have been doing was going into the room and setting eyes on this very vulnerable young patient.

Christine's body was discovered by a nurse on the morning shift, and it was clear that this patient had been dead for quite some time, and certainly a lot longer than fifteen minutes. In fact, as her post-mortem would reveal, Christine had passed away more than five hours before she was found. She was aged just twenty-two.

After knocking again on the family's front door the junior doctor and I were eventually let into the house, where it was left to me to confirm to Christine's mum and grandmother that their worst fears had come true.

'You killed her!' her mother spat, her face contorted in grief and rage. 'I knew it! Why did nobody listen to me?'

Christine's death was avoidable and I was still struggling to take in how we had failed her so catastrophically. My colleague and I both offered our deepest condolences before leaving as quickly as we could, Christine's grandmother hurling abuse at us as we walked away from the house.

When we arrived back on the unit we were told that Christine's mother had phoned up to ask if she and Granny could come in and see her old room, which still contained all of her belongings. It seemed like a reasonable request; Christine was in the morgue now, and what harm could it do? Unfortunately, the senior manager who had prevented them from visiting was sticking to his guns, citing the fact that these relatives had a history of being rude and aggressive towards the staff. Given how devastated and furious the two women were, this was certainly a risk, but I still thought it was the wrong decision. I discussed it with the charge nurse at the time – a very compassionate colleague – and Trevor agreed to turn a blind eye and let Christine's family members into the unit regardless of the orders from above. In our opinion they needed to see where she had died, and denying them this wish was unnecessarily cruel.

I'm so glad we followed our hearts. Christine's mum and granny were very grateful, and they caused no trouble at all when they came in, sitting quietly in her room and thanking Trevor for allowing this to happen. I like to think it brought them at least some solace.

The nurses who failed Christine moved to another unit before long, a decision they took themselves, knowing that management would probably have made this happen sooner rather than later in any case.

By contrast, I heard a story recently that reminded me of Christine, though the outcome was very different for everyone involved. In this case a young woman from an open psychiatric unit was picked up by the police in the town centre, where she was causing trouble late at night. She refused to engage with the officers or even give her name, and so she ended up spending the night in the cells before they worked out where she came from. The patient was returned to the unit the next morning with a caution for causing a breach of the peace. No harm had come to her and she was ultimately unscathed by her ordeal. However, the team of nurses on shift that night did not get off so lightly, and with very good reason. Every one of them was sacked after it was found that the patient had been recorded as being fast asleep in her bed the whole night long.

Orla was another patient who made a profound impact on me. I met her in 1989 when I was doing a twelve-week placement in a medium-secure unit, one of the final parts of my three-year mental health nurse training course. To get on the course I'd bought all the textbooks and taught myself to pass the five required O levels, and I couldn't wait for the day when I could finally call myself Staff Nurse Gibson. This was a much smaller facility than I was used to, but the set-up and practices were very similar to those at the big hospital.

I heard the familiar crunch of police officers' boots on lino as the double doors were unlocked and the new arrival was led onto the ward, but this time the lack of any kerfuffle caught my attention. When I looked up, I saw that our latest patient was a tall, rangy woman who had her hands cuffed behind her back and was surrounded by six burly male officers. It was usually only patients with a history of violence, or ones who were resisting or trying to escape, who had such a heavy mob of officers accompanying them. However, this patient wasn't making a sound or protesting in any way at all. She was moving slowly but deliberately in step with the officers. I was intrigued to find out her history.

The other patients on this all-female ward looked on, a mixture of boredom and disappointment etched on their faces. A new arrival normally provided a bit of entertainment to break up the monotony of the day. Shouting, struggling and hurling abuse at anyone who would listen was bog-standard behaviour but there was no such sideshow here; it was as quiet a patient admission as I'd ever seen.

Unfortunately, the police knew very little about this woman, other than that her name was Orla and she had been arrested after running down an airport runway, ripping off her clothes and shouting in her strong Irish accent that a bomb was about to explode. Coincidentally, Orla had been found at the same airport where Sister Kane had dragged the sack on the runway during one of her manic episodes. That's where the similarities ended, though, as everyone at the old asylum knew Sister Kane's medical history inside out, whereas this patient was such an unknown quantity she might as well have come from Mars. She looked to be in her mid-thirties, but that was only a guess, because Orla had no identifying documents – we couldn't find a single medical record for her and she was refusing to say a word to anybody.

We needed to build a therapeutic relationship with Orla, to gain her trust and coax her into opening up. As ever, that way we could give her the best possible care and treatment plan, and ideally start to improve her quality of life as much as possible.

'Shall we play draughts?' I said brightly.

Orla gave me a glorious smile, which she did every day.

'I'm not good at many games, but I'm *very* good at draughts!' I told her, giving her a big smile back. 'You need to be on your toes!'

As I opened the box she looked straight at me with her piercing blue eyes, and then we set out our pieces. Orla had been on the ward for several weeks now but still hadn't spoken to anyone. Like many of the nurses, I was regularly washing and blow-drying her auburn hair, taking her for walks in the secure garden and playing games with her. All of these things were designed to show her we were on her side, and that we cared. 'We're here to help,' I always reminded her. 'If there's anything you need, you can ask me. If there's something bothering you, tell me and I can try to sort it out, OK?'

Orla would nod and smile back, but her lips stayed tightly sealed.

Though she played draughts willingly, I got the impression Orla didn't care whether she won or lost. Still, I made sure she beat me from time to time, and congratulated her when she did.

'Well done! I'm determined to beat you next time! Shall we play again tomorrow?'

Despite her continued silence I kept on chatting and asking

questions, convinced it was only a matter of time before Orla would say something back. After all, we knew she had a voice, and a loud, Irish one at that. She couldn't keep this up forever.

The clinical view from the psychiatrists was that Orla must have psychosis, given she was experiencing delusions and paranoia about the IRA attempting to bomb the airport. They also thought Orla's unwillingness to talk demonstrated that she might be hearing voices that were telling her not to speak to us, that we couldn't be trusted, or we were 'the enemy'. But of course, it was all conjecture. With no medical records to go on, and zero communication from Orla, her diagnosis was really only their best guess.

Personally, I didn't agree that she saw us as the enemy, because I didn't think Orla would sit and play draughts with me or let me wash her hair if she didn't trust me, but who was I to argue? The psychiatrists (almost exclusively male; I've worked with only one female psychiatrist in forty years) held all the power, just as they did at the big hospital.

Orla never caused any trouble, complying with everything we asked her to do, and usually giving us her lovely smile as she did so. At the very start she had tried to resist taking her anti-psychotic medication, struggling to get away when she was told it was time for her injection. The doctors had put her on a slow-release 'depot' injection that would last for a week. This is given in the top part of the buttock through a large syringe and it hurts, a lot. Patients would feel sore and uncomfortable afterwards, sometimes for several days, and they would often complain that they were only just getting over the last one when the next injection was given.

Understandably, there wasn't a lot of smiling from Orla on the days she had her injection, but even so she soon stopped resisting, which I thought was revealing.

'She *must* have come into contact with mental health services in the past,' I said to Jackie, one of the night nurses who was usually coming on duty as I was finishing my regular day shift.

Jackie nodded, both of us agreeing that Orla probably knew that resistance would be futile, because she would be given the medication whether she wanted it or not. Patients who tried to run away were restrained by several nurses or, in some cases, sat on while the injection was planted in their buttock. Ultimately there was no escape, no matter how persistent you were. The patient never won, so you might as well give up without a fight. I thought Orla must have learned this from past experience, but where and why had she been sectioned before?

It was very early on an icy winter's morning when I arrived on the unit feeling frozen to the bone. I was still rubbing my hands together to try to warm myself up when Jackie called me over.

'Come and have a look at this,' she said, widening her eyes and pointing them in the direction of Orla's bedroom. 'She's been doing this all night. It's a sight to behold.'

I followed Jackie into Orla's room and my already cold body gave an involuntary little shiver. Orla was fast asleep, but instead of being in bed, she was lying on the floor in her pyjamas, her head in the open wardrobe and her long legs sticking out into the room. And when I say her head was *in* the wardrobe, I mean it was floating in thin air, as if she were sleeping on an imaginary pillow.

After six years of working in secure hospitals I thought I was beyond being surprised by anything the patients did, but I'd never seen anything like this. It was indeed a sight to behold, and quite a disturbing one too. I looked back at Jackie, my eyes like saucers.

'Catalepsy,' she said, arching her heavily plucked eyebrows.

I knew from my textbooks that catalepsy is a feature of schizophrenia, one that causes a loss of sensation and consciousness and makes the body go rigid. It means you can hold yourself in unnatural and apparently gravity-defying positions like this as you sleep. But knowing the theory is one thing; seeing it with your own eyes is quite another.

I looked around Orla's room and felt a pang of sorrow for her. Like all the bedrooms in this low-ceilinged, dark and soulless modern unit, it looked more like a prison cell than a hospital room. Orla's metal bed frame was fixed to the floor and the wardrobe and bedside table were bolted firmly to the walls, a precaution designed to stop the patients barricading themselves in their rooms or hiding behind the furniture. It was such a sad little room, and the sight of Orla with her head floating in the wardrobe made it sadder still.

Orla had been under Level 3 one-to-one observations since she was admitted, meaning she had to be in sight of a mental health nurse at all times, night and day. Given that they knew so little about her, or what risks she might pose to herself or other people, the doctors had no choice but to take this precaution. Dozens of calls to social services, local courts, police stations and probation services had failed to produce a single shred of information about her. By this point she had been with us for almost two months, yet still nobody had managed to get a single word out of her.

The night nurses took it in turns to sit outside Orla's room with the door ajar, passing a red card to the next nurse who took over. The nurse with the red card couldn't move until she was relieved by the next colleague on shift, ensuring that Orla was being permanently watched.

Jackie told me that each nurse on duty that night had moved Orla back to her bed several times. She never complained, but as soon as the nurse sat back down in the doorway, Orla got up, returned to the wardrobe and slept, trance-like, on her imaginary pillow once again.

Orla began to assume this position every night, putting the nurses through the same rigmarole of helping her back to bed only to see her return to the wardrobe again and again. After a couple of weeks and much discussion, the doctors agreed it was fruitless putting her back in bed and that she should be allowed to sleep how she chose. I thought that was the right decision. It was clearly important to Orla to sleep with her head in the wardrobe, and the thinking was that if the night nurses showed her they recognised this and respected her wishes, it might help us to gain her trust.

'I reckon we'll make a breakthrough soon,' I said to Jonathan, one evening at home. Orla had thrashed me at draughts that day and afterwards she didn't just smile at me, she almost let out a laugh.

'We're *that* close,' I said. 'I just know she's going to say something soon.'

'You're an eternal optimist, Belinda,' Jonathan replied, rolling his eyes at me, as he often did.

'I'll take that as a compliment,' I laughed. 'You have to be an optimist to do this job. I couldn't do it if I wasn't.'

Jonathan had no answer to that, because it's a truth we'd both acknowledged many times before. You simply have to look on the bright side as a mental health nurse – the alternative is to sink in a pool of gloom and despair.

Orla had been on the unit for about ten weeks when she was moved off Level 3 one-to-one observations and onto 'normal'. This meant her whereabouts and activities during the day were documented hourly and she was observed once every two hours throughout the night rather than constantly. Her bedroom door would be closed from now on, and the night nurse would observe Orla through the clear viewing window that was fitted in every patient's door.

Decisions like this weren't taken lightly. Every week, during his ward round, Orla's psychiatrist spoke to her key worker, any other doctors involved in her care, the junior doctor, a psychologist, the occupational therapist plus the art or music therapists who might have worked with Orla. Normally, this large cast of professionals would also speak with the patient themselves before making a change to their care plan, but of course Orla was still electing to say nothing.

All things considered, the psychiatrist decided Orla didn't appear to be a risk to herself or to anyone else, and a decision like this was all about risk. Orla hadn't even spoken to another patient, let alone got into an argument with anyone. She was quiet and compliant and showed no signs of self-harm or wanting to escape. Normal observations were therefore appropriate, the psychiatrist decreed. I was pleased, as it seemed the humane way to go. Up until now Orla hadn't even been allowed to go to the toilet without having a nurse at arm's length from her. Perhaps if she had more privacy, and therefore recovered some dignity, she would feel more comfortable and more inclined to open up?

It was the final week of my three-month-long placement and I was thinking about Orla on my way into work. She'd been on the unit for almost the same length of time as me, and I was desperately hoping for a breakthrough before I returned to the old hospital to complete my training.

Even though we'd never had a conversation, I felt I'd got to know Orla, in a way, and I'd developed quite a soft spot for her. Her smile always cheered me up, and I could tell when she was enjoying a game, or seemed to be at ease in my company, which was always gratifying. I really wanted to help her, and if only she would speak and allow us to understand her problems, I knew we could all help her so much more. The thought of saying goodbye and leaving her in the same state I'd met her in was dispiriting, but my time on the unit was running out fast.

I'd just bought some new nail varnish from the Avon catalogue.

It was pearly pink and I decided I was going to offer Orla a manicure today, in the hope it might work some magic on her. On the ward, my own nails were cut short and scrubbed clean – nurses were not allowed to wear jewellery or have painted nails and, unlike today, we all stuck doggedly to the rules, lest we face the wrath of a strict sister who would 'have our guts for garters'.

When I came onto the unit I went straight to the day room to say hello to the patients. Orla sat in the same chair every morning after breakfast, but today it was empty.

'Where's Orla?' I asked, looking around.

'Oh, don't you know?' one of the older male nurses said. 'She's dead.'

I was stunned, my breath catching in my throat.

'What? When?'

I'd been away for a long weekend, but even so, how could this have happened in such a short period of time? I was absolutely horrified.

'She strangled herself,' he went on. 'Jackie found her. Let me think. Saturday, early hours, it must have been. She was found with her head in the wardrobe.'

With that the nurse scuttled off to attend to a patient who was shouting his name. He wasn't being uncaring; I understood he was rushed off his feet and had no time to stop. There had been no question of anyone taking me to one side to break it to me gently; it was never like that when there was bad news. Orla was dead, and mental health nurses like us just had to keep going. We were there to take care of those who were living, and there was no time to spare.

I went to Orla's room and was shocked all over again. It was empty, all trace of her removed. I spoke to another nurse, and she told me there had been no change in Orla's behaviour in the hours before she killed herself. She had gone to sleep in the wardrobe as usual, and when she was sure she was not being observed she managed to strangle herself with a bed sheet, using the clothes rail as a ligature point. You had to go into the room to be able to look inside the wardrobe and see Orla's head floating, but her legs always told us what was happening. Or at least they had, up until now. When the night nurse looked through the viewing window her suspicions weren't aroused, because Orla looked to be in the same position as always, with her legs protruding from the wardrobe and her head inside.

There were so many questions I would never know the answer to. Had this been Orla's plan all along, or did she spot an opportunity to kill herself on the spur of the moment? Most of all, was there anything we could have done to prevent this outcome?

I got on with my day, still reeling with shock but too busy to discuss Orla with any other colleagues.

A couple of days later, at the end of my shift, a very young nursing assistant came dashing towards me, looking and sounding incredibly upset.

'Belinda, oh, Belinda!' she wailed.

'It's so sad, isn't it?' I said, assuming she wanted to talk about Orla, who was still looming large in my mind.

'Sad?' she frowned.

Cheryl was red in the face, breathing heavily, and seemed to be on hot pins. Clearly, she was talking about something else entirely.

'What? What is it?'

'It's Hank,' she gasped. 'Haven't you heard?'

'No. What's happened?'

'He's driving my boyfriend's car! I'm beside myself! This is awful!'

Hank was a middle-aged patient with a diagnosis of schizophrenia. He'd been brought into the unit after half-heartedly holding up a post office with a child's plastic gun, insisting it was on the orders of his 'gangland leaders'. Now, somehow, the six-foot-tall, eighteen-stone patient had slipped out unnoticed when Cheryl's boyfriend Duncan popped up to the ward to tell her he'd arrived to collect her at the end of her shift. Duncan had left his keys in the ignition of his Ford Escort, Cheryl explained, which was something he was in the habit of doing.

'It's a catastrophe!'

I gave Cheryl a hug. Just seventeen, she reminded me of myself at that age, in a permanent state of shock and awe at everything she was seeing and learning. I established that security staff and a group of the unit's burliest male nurses were already outside, desperately trying to stop Hank from doing loop after loop around the unit, driving over flowerbeds and sending startled pedestrians scattering.

'Will I get the sack?' Cheryl asked, wiping tears from her cheeks.

'No, no,' I soothed. 'We're all human, mistakes happen. It looks like Hank's seized an opportunity, that's all. It's not your fault.'

An image of Orla in the wardrobe flickered across my mind.

She had died under our collective care, but life on the unit had resumed, just like that. We had done our best, but sometimes patients beat us at our own game.

The suicide of a patient isn't common in forensic nursing, precisely because of the high levels of observation in place, although as Orla demonstrated, it can and does happen. Sometimes patients are so determined to take their own life they are willing to play a long game, and they have all the time in the world to observe the nursing staff. I came to think that Orla had lulled us into a false sense of security about her safety, and when she was sure she wouldn't be interrupted, she had put her plan into action.

Hank, meanwhile, drove around the unit for three hours, until the car ran out of petrol and he was escorted back inside. A couple of the nurses speculated over what he would say about it afterwards. Perhaps he had been following orders from his 'gangland bosses' again, and maybe he thought Duncan's Ford Escort was the getaway car?

The truth was far more mundane. Hank had noticed that Duncan always left his keys in the ignition. He'd been keeping his eyes peeled for days and, as I'd suspected, he'd simply grabbed the opportunity when it presented itself to him. The observed had become the observer, just as in poor Orla's case.

Looking back, Orla's was the most shocking, unusual and inexplicable suicide I've ever experienced. The fact that I was working so closely with her in the days and months leading up to her death and did not see it coming at all made it extremely hard for me to deal with. I was devastated for a long, long time, and I will never forget her. Her death remains a source of sadness to this day.

With the exception of Orla, the suicidal patients I've encountered have generally fallen into one of three categories.

There are what's known as 'parasuicidal' people who carry out 'cry for help' acts but don't really want to die. Then you have patients like Alfred and Shirley who simply do not want to be here any more, and this feeling does not pass over time. Thankfully, they are in the minority. Much more common, in my experience, are the patients who firmly believe they want to kill themselves at a particular moment in time, but with the proper support and care that feeling passes. Given her bipolar disorder, I think Sister Kane fell into this category, and with the right help at the right time, she might not have taken her own life. We can never know for sure, but I believe that to be the case. It's a thought that brings little comfort when I picture Sister Kane's happy face and admiring patients. But then I remind myself how much has changed over the decades in mental health, and how this majority group of suicidal people are now treated with far more understanding, and given talking therapy alongside improved medication, not to mention the correct support at work.

I'm sure Sister Kane would raise a glass of Babycham, or perhaps a snowball, to the progress we have made, and the lives that have been saved.

CHAPTER 3

'Whatever the patients have done, you have to treat them all the same way'

Nikolajs took my hand in his and kissed it chivalrously, as he did every day. He was a charming old boy, the type who looked like the archetypal granddad in an advert for toffees or cosy slippers.

'How are you?' I asked cheerily, enjoying seeing the twinkle in his silver-grey eyes.

'Goo,' he said in his strong Latvian accent.

A survivor of a Nazi concentration camp, Nikolajs had arrived in England as a refugee after the Second World War. His English was very limited, but he always tipped his head and smiled sweetly at me from his plastic seat in the smaller of the two lounges on Ward 14. He would stay in the same place all day long, watching other patients play pool and saying virtually nothing, always with the same kind, contented smile on his face.

Seth, an ex-miner who had spent the whole of his working life down the pit, sat beside him every day. His forehead was creased in a permanent frown as he leaned forward on his walking stick, making up for Nikolajs's silence by constantly complaining in his broad Yorkshire accent.

'That's my bloody chair!' I'd hear him shout as I approached the lounge. 'Get on!'

It was a familiar cry. Woe betide anyone who sat in the wing-backed, faded burgundy plastic seat Seth had made his own. I often wondered why Nikolajs allowed him to sit next to him, or didn't move somewhere else, because it seemed like the worst place on the ward for such a quiet, gentle soul to be.

'Get on, lad!' Seth continued, waving his stick at a teenage boy called Billy who had been admitted to the unit the night before.

In the handover earlier that morning I'd learned that Billy had ended up with us after a store detective at Superdrug caught him stealing a packet of Walkers cheese and onion crisps. The police put him in a cell overnight and presented him to the magistrates' court the next day, and as he couldn't provide an address he was remanded to a local prison. Billy had been in and out of open psychiatric wards for years and it was obvious he had some significant mental health problems, so after a brief spell on the prison's psychiatric wing he had been transferred to us for assessment.

'Poor lad,' I thought. 'If anyone could do without rattling Seth's cage, it's this boy.'

I watched as Billy scuttled off towards the toilets, looking back over his shoulder as he quickened his pace. His panic-filled eyes were darting everywhere, as if he were looking for a sniper lurking behind one of the murky windows lining the long corridor.

The heavy toilet doors always banged loudly as they were opened and shut and I saw Billy jump out of his skin when he heard the sound blast like a gunshot down the narrow passageway.

'I know what tha's doin' down there!' Seth yelled after him. 'And *you* can go in that coffin!'

My heart went out to Billy and as soon as I got the chance I made sure to tell him this was not the personal threat it seemed. I explained that Seth shouted out (and sometimes screamed) the same thing every time the toilet doors banged, because he was under the long-held illusion that the nurses were busy building him a coffin in the bathroom.

'What?' Billy said, still looking for invisible snipers. 'A coffin? He's tapped!'

I couldn't help disliking Seth a little bit more every time I saw him making someone else's day that much worse. Like Nikolajs, he was already an old man when I met him on my first day on Ward 14. Well into his seventies, he was now shrunken, frail and increasingly skinny, but Seth's nastiness and bigotry were as robust as they'd ever been.

He had a habit of treating all the female staff with unfiltered contempt and was clearly of the opinion that women were inferior to men and only useful to bring him food and drinks and perform other menial tasks.

'When's me dinner coming?' he'd whine, shaking his stick at us as we served the school-dinner-style minced beef and mash from the trolley we wheeled into the dining room. 'Get on with it, woman!'

One day we got so fed up with Seth's stick-waving we took it off him, though when we realised that this meant one of us needed to support him every time he moved around the ward we soon gave it back.

Seth never said thank you for anything, though when our nursing officer, Mr Woodhead, came onto the ward he suddenly found not only some manners, but plenty of charm too. It was like a switch was thrown, the frown lifting from Seth's face as he magically unhunched himself from his stick and allowed the corners of his mouth to rise.

'It's always a pleasure to see you, Mr Woodhead,' he'd say, adjusting the spectacles on the end of his thin nose before striking up a lively conversation about the running of the hospital, or Maggie Thatcher and the miners' strike. Complaints about the female nurses were always another hot topic. I noticed that even when his hard-working staff were being criticised Mr Woodhead listened attentively to Seth's gripes. It seemed to me that our nursing officer enjoyed the fact he was the only person Seth spoke to in any meaningful way. I found this very annoying, although admittedly there was never any love lost between me and Mr Woodhead. Not long after I started work on the ward Mr Woodhead came over and asked me to make him a cup of tea. I was in the middle of playing cards with Nikolajs and so I handed him the keys to the kitchen and told him to make it himself. I didn't react when he shook his head at me and marched off the ward, his big red face shining a bit brighter that morning.

Another of Seth's irritating habits was to share his cigarettes with other patients, but only the men, of course, and typically those who were the biggest and strongest on the ward. However, Seth's worst trait by a long chalk was the shameless way he bragged about the reason he had been detained for so many years.

Seth had killed his wife, Jenny, and he would tell his story often and loudly, always with an odious note of macho pride in his voice, and without any hint of remorse. The details were shocking and never became less so in repetition. It didn't take long for me to know the tale off by heart, having heard it from the horse's mouth as well as from reading his files.

Poor Jenny had endured a dreadful life with Seth, who physically abused her and was unfaithful throughout their long marriage. In her middle age she had a habit of stripping down to her vest and washing herself at the sink in the kitchen, which irritated Seth no end. He got it into his head that she was trying to show off her body to the young man who lived across the street, and one day Seth couldn't take it any more.

'She didn't know her place,' he would scowl as he reached the climax of his story. Cool as a cucumber, Seth walked into the kitchen, picked up a carving knife and stabbed Jenny to death as she stood at the sink in her underwear. 'I'm innocent, Seth,' she shouted, but her desperate protest didn't stop her husband from coldly taking her life.

After stabbing Jenny, Seth calmly picked up a mirror and held it to her mouth as she lay on the kitchen floor, making sure his wife was no longer breathing before calling the police.

A tape recording of his 999 call was played at his trial. 'I've killed me wife,' Seth said matter-of-factly. 'Don't call an ambulance because she's already dead.' He attempted to hang up the phone but the operator was still on the line, preventing him from ending the call. Seth was very annoyed. 'I've told you she's dead,' he said impatiently. 'I held a mirror up to her mouth and she were not breathing. I know she's dead, so can you get off the line because I want to phone me brother!'

The court heard that Seth had been diagnosed with a rare paranoid syndrome specifically linked to his wife, and his lawyer successfully argued that he had acted with diminished responsibility. Given that at the time of the killing he was already a pensioner, and that his diagnosis meant he was only a threat to Jenny, detention in a secure unit was considered the most appropriate option.

I worked with Seth right up until Ward 14 was shut down at the start of the 1990s, though in my experience he never showed signs of having a severe mental health diagnosis. The paranoid delusions he had about nurses building a coffin did nothing to convince me otherwise. It's very unusual to have delusions about only one thing while displaying no other symptoms of mental ill-health, though it was not my job to question a diagnosis and I would not have been listened to even if I had. I was employed to nurse Seth, and it was my responsibility to do so with the same care, compassion and respect I showed every other patient on the ward.

Nurse Felicity Stockwell's study *The Unpopular Patient* was published in 1972, its findings challenging the consensus that nurses necessarily treated all patients equally and in a non-judgemental manner. After examining the work of general nurses, Nurse Stockwell found that the quality of care given to a patient was directly related to their popularity, those who were bad-tempered, grumbling or who were perceived to be taking a hospital bed unnecessarily being viewed as 'difficult' and given a lower standard of treatment and care.

The pattern continues to this day, and in my experience patients arriving at A & E after self-harming or attempting suicide often come off worst, being treated unkindly by doctors and nurses who are working under acute pressure. I've seen patients having wounds stitched without pain relief and overdose patients being treated like time-wasters who are stealing resources from patients who are 'really' in need of attention. But a parasuicide attempt is a psychiatric emergency, and as such it should be treated in the same way as a heart attack or any other physical emergency, whatever the staff think and however much pressure they are under.

My mental health nurse training involved a huge amount of work on improving self-awareness, recognising our own prejudices and trying to identify our subconscious biases and blind spots. The 'Johari Window Model' (developed in 1955 by the American psychologists Joseph Luft and Harry Ingham – hence the name) encouraged us to better understand our relationship with ourselves and others. We were instructed to look at four areas of ourselves (ranging from blind spots and the 'hidden' and 'unknown' areas to our 'open' self), the point being to identify our weaknesses, recognise to what extent we were aware of them and strive to increase the 'open' area, where self-awareness is at its peak and we have the deepest possible understanding of ourselves, our beliefs and our values. I learned that this level of self-knowledge is invaluable in developing the 'non-judgemental self', which is a vitally important skill for the mental health nurse when building a therapeutic relationship. Behaving in a non-judgemental way means listening to the patient in an empathetic manner, showing understanding, not making assumptions and putting your own judgements and values to one side, no matter what you are confronted with. In theory, when you've successfully developed your non-judgemental self you can work in a therapeutic manner with any patient – murderers and other extremely unlikeable patients like Seth included.

Not every nurse succeeds, and some don't even get off first base.

For part of the training course we all had to do a placement on the large dementia unit of the hospital. In those days the focus was on 'reality orientation' which involved, amongst other things, having large clocks around the ward with the date and time on, as well as signs, labels and pictures on cupboards and doors to remind patients where the kitchen or bathroom was, or where to hang their dressing gown, and so on.

One of the patients was a very gentle old lady called Mabel who had been admitted to the ward following the death of her husband Edward, a devoted man who had been caring for his wife at home for many years. Mabel had quite advanced dementia and wandered around all day long, calling for Edward and asking everyone, 'Have you seen my husband? Where is he?' This behaviour increased around teatime when Mabel expected Edward to be home from work.

Nowadays we would try to distract a patient like Mabel and focus on the underlying feeling of worry she was experiencing, but back then it was a case of trying to remind her of the reality. 'Mabel, your husband is not here,' we'd say gently. 'Edward is no longer with us. I'm afraid he passed away, but you're safe here with us. We are looking after you.'

However we said it, this news would send Mabel into floods of tears before she would begin again with, 'Where is my husband? Do you know when he will be back?'

The majority of the trainees, myself included, instinctively changed tack after a while, recognising that putting Mabel through this again and again was clearly pointless and causing her unnecessary distress. 'Shall I walk with you to the lounge?' I'd say. 'Let's see who's in there, shall we?'

One of the other students on my course was a middle-aged man called Patrick who'd tried various jobs, the last one being a bus driver, before deciding to train as a mental health nurse. He stuck out like a sore thumb amongst all the bright-eyed twenty-somethings, always looking very awkward in his tartan sports jacket and black slacks. It seems cruel now, but the young men in the class nicknamed him 'Pervy Patrick', something all the girls laughed at. So much for learning to recognise our blind spots and relinquish our unconscious bias, but I'm afraid it was another era, and we had an awful lot to learn. When it came to dealing with Mabel it's fair to say Patrick didn't have a clue. He persisted in telling her in no uncertain terms that Edward was dead, and he did it in an increasingly forthright manner.

'I told you yesterday!' I heard him say, exasperated. 'He's dead, woman! You're not going to find him here or anywhere else!'

Presumably none of our superiors witnessed Patrick's interactions with Mabel because this continued for weeks, until one day Patrick presented the patient with a freshly printed colour photograph.

'Look!' he said, thrusting the photo in Mabel's face. 'This is Edward's grave. Look at it. He is dead. He is not here. He is never coming back, so you need to stop looking for him!'

Patrick then proceeded to show her a whole set of pictures of Edward's grave, photographed from different angles. Mabel's face crumpled and she sobbed her heart out as she stared at image after image.

When word got round the rest of us were naturally horrified, but Patrick couldn't understand what the problem was at all, explaining with some pride how he'd gone to the trouble of finding Edward's grave and taken not just one, but a whole reel of photographs to show Mabel the reality of the situation. He'd then gone to Boots the Chemists to have the film developed, at his own expense, no less. 'It's reality orientation at its finest, this is,' he said.

A few days later Patrick was humiliated in class by one of our nurse tutors, who got us all to stand up and form a 'human sculpture' showing how she saw the group. All the young men, excluding Patrick, were put in a group with their arms held out towards the girls, and us women were put in another group, stretching our arms out towards the boys. Patrick was placed a long way away from both groups, looking out of the window and with his back towards the rest of the class.

'I see the boys as a cohesive group and the girls as a cohesive group who are connected to each other,' the nurse tutor said. 'I see Patrick as not connected to any group, looking out of the window and thinking, "What the hell am I doing here?"'

I was immature enough to laugh along with my peers at this too, though in hindsight the nurse tutor was quite mean to put him through that. Patrick had struggled throughout the course to connect with his peers, let alone show that he understood how to form a therapeutic relationship with any of the patients. He chose to leave the course soon afterwards, a decision that would have been made for him if he hadn't made it himself.

In years to come I often thought of Patrick if ever I struggled to form a therapeutic relationship with a patient. Without wanting to rub yet more salt in the man's wounds, his story would remind me that I *did* have what it took, even though with some people I cared for it wasn't always easy to suspend all judgement.

Seth tested my skills to the limit, and there were many times when I had to bite my tongue and remind myself of good nursing practice, shown to me and handed down by Ena, Sister Kane, Neil, my tutors and many others. 'Is your nursing practice of a standard you would be happy for your loved one to receive? Reflect on your practice. What went well? What didn't? What needs to change? Be mindful and present in your interactions with patients. Really listen to them, and keep listening.' All of those wise words helped me care for Seth. Granted, I might have given Nikolajs the better-looking mug of tea from time to time, and my smile might have slipped off my face occasionally when I turned away from Seth, but I don't think he was ever any the wiser. I hope not.

I've nursed several other patients who have been accused of murder, killed someone or been involved in the death of another human being, some more difficult to care for than others. The following stand out in my memory.

'Not again,' I thought, seeing a cowering Gary being escorted onto the ward by two police officers who each towered at least a foot above him. As usual Gary's face was bright red due to the vast amounts of petrol he sniffed on a regular basis, typically stolen from people's cars.

'Hi,' he said sheepishly, catching my eye.

'Hello, Gary,' I said. 'You can release him now, officers. I can take it from here, thanks.'

Gary gave me a grateful smile. 'How are you doing?' he asked, in the way the black sheep of the family might cautiously approach a parent when he returned to the fold.

'Fine, thank you for asking,' I said, giving him a smile back. I wanted to add that I was sorry to see him here again, but something stopped me. For one thing I'd just started my shift and didn't know what the story was this time, or whether it really was such a bad thing for Gary.

'It's not that bad,' he said, as if reading my mind.

I'd known Gary for so many years that he really did feel like a member of my extended family. He visibly relaxed when the door to the unit locked behind the police officers, and I found myself sharing some of his very palpable relief. Ward 14 was a place where Gary was well known, where people treated him well, and it was also probably the only place in the world where he'd ever felt safe.

Gary's life was very sad. Sexually abused from a young age, he was now a small, thin and conventionally unattractive young man in his twenties, unwanted and unloved by his family and living unhappily in a supported hostel. In those days we probably would have described Gary as being 'a bit dim' and having 'short-man syndrome' too, neither of which helped him to be accepted in the community. Add to that the fact he was a thief and had an aggressive streak, and it was easy to see how Gary had found himself living such a lonely, miserable existence. It's very sad to say it, but nobody liked Gary, and he had nobody.

Time and again Gary would go missing from the hostel and

then behave aggressively towards the police officers who picked him up on the streets. They would once again detain him under the Mental Health Act and bring him to us for a short stay, whereupon he'd fall into yet another all-too-familiar and disconcerting cycle.

'Gary, we're planning to discharge you by the end of the week.'

I always dreaded his reaction when I told him that. Though he was usually quite friendly and chatty towards the staff and other patients for most of his stay, at the mention of being discharged Gary's face would fall and he'd become moody and defensive. 'What d'ya mean? You can't do that! I'm not well. Where will I go? Can't I stay a bit longer? Please let me stay.'

He'd usually try to pick an unimaginative argument with someone on the ward, typically a person who was an easy target, like Victor the pub singer when he was singing one of his favourite Elton John or Billy Joel classics.

'You're murdering that song,' Gary would mutter, wanting to create disharmony but not quite brave enough to start a proper fight. Victor's lip would curl and he'd threaten to box Gary's ears, but being the decent man he was he never carried out his threat.

All the staff had got wise to Gary's goading and delaying tactics and we knew we had to be extra vigilant in the run-up to his discharge, not least because he had another trick up his sleeve, and I mean that only too literally. Gary was a self-harmer, which became another one of the reasons he was frequently sectioned and brought back to us.

During this latest stay Marie, a very persistent self-harmer, taunted Gary about the tiny silver scars on the upper side of his forearms. 'That's pathetic,' she said. 'Is that all you've got?'

Unfortunately, Gary's response to Marie's competitive criticism was to slash his arm from the wrist to the shoulder, using the blade he took from a safety razor that he managed to convince another patient to 'lend' him. This was a not-uncommon tactic used by self-harmers on the ward, but unfortunately it was one we struggled to prevent, given that patients had to be allowed to shave and it was not feasible or desirable to observe every patient around the clock, both for practical and psychological reasons. The gaping wound needed fifty stitches, which were given without anaesthetic by a tutting A & E doctor, while Gary did an unconvincing job of pretending he could easily cope with the excruciating pain.

After that we worked more intensively with Gary than we had before. As soon as he was physically fit enough, a community-based programme was put in place to keep him engaged throughout the week, including swimming on a Monday, food shopping and cooking back on the unit on a Tuesday, a support group for people with addiction problems at the church hall on Wednesdays, and so on. The hope was that these activities and supportive measures would help Gary manage his emotional needs, and that once he was discharged he would continue with at least some of the activities.

To start with, one of our nurses accompanied Gary into the community, but as the weeks went by and he was doing well, this support was gradually withdrawn so that he attended his activities independently, returning to the ward at the end of each day. However, once Gary started doing 'too well', at least in his view, he began to self-sabotage. This involved some deliberate but relatively minor acts of self-harm, such as making tiny cuts on his arms, and a series of petty thefts, typically shoplifting, very obviously in sight of a store detective. When the police were called, and once the store detective had explained the nature of the theft, Gary would be escorted back to the ward by a couple of officers.

A psychologist worked with Gary twice a week to help him manage his self-harm, and he had a weekly session with a probation officer to focus on minimising his offending behaviour. There were also weekly multidisciplinary team meetings attended by the world and her husband, including police and probation officers, a psychologist, an occupational therapist, a psychiatrist and some members of the nursing staff, all of whom scrutinised Gary's care plan and made sure it was working for him. Suffice to say, everybody wanted Gary to succeed in being discharged and living a positive life in the community. Everybody, that is, except Gary himself. It had become abundantly clear that he enjoyed the care and security the locked ward provided, and that he wanted to be with his 'family', because that is exactly what I and many other nurses had effectively become to him.

One night, when he was staying overnight in his hostel – something we were encouraging – Gary deliberately started a fire in the metal waste bin in his bedroom. He'd done this several times in the past, and he also had a history of accidentally starting fires at the hostel when he sniffed petrol and decided to light a cigarette. He knew he was in the last chance saloon when it came to fire-starting, accidental or otherwise, and of course he was kicked out of the hostel once and for all.

When he arrived back at the unit we routinely took his matches and lighters off him, as we did with all patients, even though we knew that Gary would never dream of committing arson on the ward. It was the very last thing he would do, because Gary knew full well what starting a fire would mean. We could never admit him to Ward 14 again, and he would have to move up the secure chain to a medium-secure hospital.

A room in a new hostel was found for Gary and over the following months and years the same frustrating cycle continued with a vengeance, with Gary coming in and out of the ward at regular intervals, doing all he could to avoid being discharged, and pressing the self-destruct button whenever he appeared to be making good progress once he was back in the community.

One night he was caught red-handed, stealing petrol from an elderly man's car at a petrol station. A fight broke out between the two of them, during which the pensioner collapsed from a heart attack and sadly died. The Crown Prosecution Service decided there wasn't enough evidence to prove Gary had been a direct cause of the pensioner's death, and as a result he escaped a charge of manslaughter.

Back on Ward 14 there were discussions between senior staff about whether Gary could stay on the secure unit on a longer-term basis. I thought this was a good idea as it might perhaps give him time to mature, but it was eventually ruled out because Gary was not diagnosed with psychosis (he was the only patient on the ward not on anti-psychotic medication) and he didn't meet the criteria for long-term detention under the Mental Health Act. Instead, a new multidisciplinary team put together another plan of care designed once again to help Gary build a better life in the community. It was as supportive, intensive and expensive as the last one, though the various professionals involved did nothing to hide the fact that they were running out of patience with Gary, and that this was going to be the last significant package of help he would receive.

In spite of his attachment to the unit, once this care plan was in place Gary successfully appealed his detention. This was something he'd done on a number of occasions in the past, taking us by surprise each time. The only explanation seemed to be that he enjoyed the attention the discharge brought him, because there would inevitably be a mad rush to find him accommodation and support in the community.

'It's attention-seeking behaviour,' some of my colleagues said dismissively.

This really got my back up. I'd come to see that there is always a reason a person wants attention, and whatever that reason might be it is unfailingly rooted in an emotional need. Therefore, accusing someone of attention-seeking means that you are being dismissive of their needs, which is quite wrong. In Gary's case he needed to be loved and cared for, or at least to know that someone was bothered about him. It was not very much to want, or to acknowledge.

Gary was eventually placed in a semi-detached house in a very bleak part of town. He was in his early thirties now. Jonathan began calling in to see him every day – he had also worked with Gary for so many years and viewed him like a member of our family. The unloved street was surrounded by derelict land and the house next door stood empty, a deliberate move given Gary's history of starting fires. The grim description made my heart sink.

'He's not bad, though,' Jonathan said. 'In fact he's doing really well, I think. But you know Gary, it's the calm before the storm.'

With help, Gary slowly started to make the house quite homely inside, though I was acutely aware that whatever he did he was ultimately alone, no doubt feeling as unloved and unwanted as he always had.

One day Jonathan arrived to find the predictable storm was brewing. Gary had smashed his way through his living-room wall and into the derelict house next door. He used an old hammer and it must have taken him hours and hours, and in the process he'd filled his home with dust and debris and made his living room uninhabitable.

'What on earth did he do that for?' I said, upset and exasperated.

'To sniff petrol next door,' Jonathan sighed.

The huge amount of support Gary was receiving was gradually being withdrawn, and we both knew it was only a matter of time before he created more damage and disruption. It was awful to have this insight and yet be powerless to prevent the inevitable, but after so many years of experience that's exactly the position Jonathan and I were in. It was not a question of *whether* Gary would reoffend, but of what he would do next in order to ensure his return to the unit.

Unfortunately, we didn't have long to wait for the answer. One night Gary sniffed petrol in his bedroom and either deliberately or accidentally set the house on fire, trapping himself upstairs. A passer-by phoned the fire brigade and a full crew of firefighters entered the burning house to rescue Gary. The blaze was extensive, the flames having spread rapidly through the building, and Gary was very lucky to escape without serious injury. He was hoping to come 'home' to the unit while the mess was sorted out, but this time it was not to be.

Not only had the wider multidisciplinary team finally lost all patience with Gary but the police decided to progress him down the criminal justice path. He was promptly remanded in custody, charged with 'intent to endanger life' and – very alarmingly – 'attempted murder of the fire brigade'.

Although he would have much preferred to be on the secure ward amongst people he knew, Gary didn't hate prison. He'd spent time inside before, on minor charges such as shoplifting, and to Gary even being detained at Her Majesty's pleasure was preferable to fending for himself in the even lonelier outside world. However, he had never faced such serious charges before, and I wondered how he would cope with what must have been a terrifying charge sheet, and the realisation that he was likely to be inside for quite some time.

After several weeks a visiting order arrived on the ward, sent by Gary from prison and addressed specifically to Jonathan and me. It prompted a debate between the two of us about whether we should discuss this with members of Gary's care team. In the end we decided not to. We were quite sure none of the senior professionals would want to join us on the visit, and we were also afraid that they might not support our decision to see Gary. It probably wasn't the wisest move on our part – it's always best to be transparent in these circumstances – but given that Jonathan and I had both built up such a strong relationship with Gary over a long period of time we felt within our rights to make up our own minds. If I'm totally honest, I was also following my heart. There had been many occasions when I considered how different Gary's life would have been had he not suffered the abuse he did in his childhood. What if he had real family to talk to and share a laugh with? What if just one person had loved him, or he had had the chance to love? Jonathan and I had all of those things and more. Paying Gary a visit was the least we could do.

Just before we set off for the prison, Jonathan took a call from the local police. An officer who knew us had spotted our dog Oliver roaming around near the canal, and she had picked him up and taken him to the police station. It had been Jonathan's idea that we should sell our first house and experience living on a narrowboat.

He'd taken a group of patients out on the canal one day and absolutely loved it, and he also thought Oliver, a thirty-kilo English Bull Terrier, would enjoy the lifestyle. It turned out we all did, the only fly in the ointment being that Oliver quickly learned how to open the doors of the narrowboat. As a result he was soon known to all and sundry – including the local police – as 'Oliver the escape artist'.

'How soon can you get here?' the police officer asked Jonathan.

'We'll come straight away,' he said, thanking her profusely.

We both agreed we were lucky the police were so accommodating – Oliver might well have ended up in the pound – and we headed straight to the station to collect him. The clock was ticking, however, and Jonathan could see I was feeling a bit stressed about missing visiting hours.

'We should have time to fetch the dog and still get to visiting,' he reassured me, though I knew he was being a tad optimistic.

'He's done worse,' Jonathan went on, distracting me with a reminder of one of Oliver's most notorious capers. 'We'll have to tell Gary this one. Or maybe not!'

The story never failed to bring a smile to my face, as Jonathan knew very well. As we drove in the opposite direction to the prison I found myself laughing, as I always did whenever I remembered the tale.

I'd taken Oliver to work with me because he wasn't very well, thinking that as I was on a night shift he could stay in the secure yard outside, where I could keep an eye on him. As it happened, when all the patients had gone to bed it was unusually quiet on the ward and so I decided there was no need to leave Oliver outside on his own.

'Now you be a good boy,' I said, sneaking him into the nurses' office.

Oliver was happy to curl up quietly in the warm room, but when a patient called Robert got up unexpectedly in the middle of the night, complaining that he couldn't sleep, Oliver was straight up on his feet, tail wagging.

'I bloody love dogs!' Robert proclaimed, immediately brightening. 'Come here, boy!'

Robert started stroking Oliver enthusiastically and the dog was lapping it up, delighted to have such a fuss made of him in the middle of the night. It was good to see, and after a little while the pair of them settled down in the corner of the room, Oliver lying contentedly at Robert's feet.

'Shall we have a hot drink?' I said, thinking I'd have a coffee and Robert could have something milky, to help him sleep.

'Grand,' he said. 'I'll watch the dog, no bother.'

Oliver was closing his eyes as I walked to the kitchen at the other end of the unit, but by the time I reached the kitchen door I could hear him barking loudly. Meanwhile, Robert was screaming and shouting at the top of his voice. I turned on my heel and ran back to the office as fast as I could, wondering what on earth had gone on. To my horror Robert was in a highly agitated state; his T-shirt had been ripped clean off his back and was lying shredded to pieces all over the floor.

'I was only play-fighting,' Robert stuttered as I grabbed hold of the overexcited dog and led him away.

There was nothing for it but to take Oliver to the car, give Robert a sedative and send him back to bed, all of which I somehow managed to do while the other members of staff on duty were otherwise engaged.

In my overnight report, left for the staff on duty the next morning, I chose my words carefully. 'Robert had a disturbed night's sleep,' I wrote, 'and talked about a dog attacking him and ripping his T-shirt.'

No questions were asked and it was left at that, nobody believing poor Robert's version of events could possibly be true.

A few days later, when I was back on days, Robert made a beeline for me.

'That dog did rip off my bloody T-shirt, didn't he, Belinda?'

I raised my eyebrows, as if to say, 'What can you do, Robert, if people don't believe you?'

I reasoned that no real harm had been done and at least lessons had been learned. Oliver was never coming to work with me again, and it was the last time Robert ever got up in the night.

Once we'd collected Oliver from the police station we had to take him back to the boat, by which time, as I'd feared, we'd completely missed visiting time at the prison.

'We'll have to wait for Gary to send us another visiting order,' Jonathan said.

'We will,' I said. 'And he will.'

We didn't receive another visiting order from Gary, though, and a few weeks after our missed opportunity we received some dreadful news.

Gary had hanged himself in prison.

I remember the immense shock of hearing the news being tempered, ever so slightly, by a deep-rooted expectation I'd carried with me for a long time, but never quite wanted to acknowledge. Death at a young age had always been a likely outcome for our Gary.

Based on the many years I'd worked with him, getting to know him very well in the process, I don't believe Gary intended to kill himself. I think it was a parasuicide attempt that went wrong, from a young man who struggled with life and needed attention.

It had not been his decision to move into the bleak house and live more independently than he had in the supported hostel, and given the choice I think Gary would have stayed where he was, or at least moved to another hostel where he would have had support. All the professionals involved in his care had his best interests at heart, but to this day I wonder if collectively we'd pushed him too hard to stand on his own two feet, and if he would still be alive today if we hadn't.

'He's not saying anything,' a female police officer told me, phoning the ward in advance of bringing Warren in. 'We've got him in a cell at the minute. He looks like the Michelin Man and he doesn't smell too good. He's been living on the streets for months.'

Nowadays it would be considered very non-PC for a police officer to make reference to a person's size, let alone compare a patient to the famously huge Michelin tyre mascot, but I didn't flinch at this description. On the contrary, I was grateful for the heads-up.

'Hello,' I said, taking in the sight and smells of Warren an hour later. His pointy-nosed, sunken face seemed too small and scrawny for his gigantic, squishy body and he smelled like the overflowing bins at the side of the kebab shop in town. I thanked our lucky stars it was winter, or goodness knows how much worse the stench would have been.

'We'll get you settled in,' I said after the officers had released him from his handcuffs and left him in our care. 'Would you like to call anyone, Warren, and let them know you are here?'

Warren bored into me with his dark, intense eyes, giving a sort of grunt and a shake of the head. I found myself feeling strangely discombobulated. By this point in my career I'd dealt with all manner of difficult patients, but there was something not right with this man – something over and above the fact he smelled so atrocious, was electing to communicate in grunts and was wearing the most enormous, dirty grey suit I'd ever seen in my life.

A couple of the male nursing assistants escorted Warren, wobbling, rustling and emitting wafts of unpleasant fumes, to the bathroom. Other patients stared suspiciously – I wondered if they had similar feelings to me.

An hour or so later I came across the same two male nursing

assistants in the corridor. This time they were taking a skinny little patient to his bedroom. He was no more than five foot two in height and had the exact same pointy-nosed, sunken face as Warren.

'Oh!' I exclaimed, the penny dropping as I asked the nurses to come and see me as soon as Warren was settled for the night.

'What on earth?' I said. 'How many clothes was he wearing to make him look that big?'

'It wasn't just clothes. He was wearing his breakfast, dinner and tea, and a lot more besides!'

The two young nurses cracked up laughing as they described in stomach-turning detail what they had discovered as they helped Warren out of his mountain of clothes. He had been wearing a total of forty items of layered clothing, including seven suits in various sizes. In between the layers were wads of scrunched-up old newspapers and bits of food including stale sandwiches, half-eaten burgers and mouldy biscuits.

'You're kidding me?'

'No!' they said, unable to stop laughing. 'Have a look if you don't believe us – there's two bin bags full of his stuff.'

I laughed along with them, feeling quite relieved. My gut instinct had been right. There certainly had been something that didn't meet the eye with Warren, but I hadn't expected that.

The next day I saw Warren in the TV lounge and went over to have a chat. 'How are you?' I asked. 'Did you have a comfortable night?'

He smelled as fresh as a daisy and was wearing a clean set of hospital-issue clothes, but the same feeling resurfaced that I'd had when he arrived. Warren made me feel strangely uneasy, though I couldn't put my finger on exactly why.

'Fine,' he grunted, staring at me with flinty, angry eyes.

A chill shot straight through me, the hairs on the back of my neck bristling.

I'd met plenty of patients who were rude, uncommunicative and tried to intimidate the staff, but I'd never once had a reaction as unsettling as this.

'He's a very dangerous man,' I thought, unable to stop the words filling my head.

Nothing about his behaviour really suggested this. Warren hadn't given the police officers a hard time when they picked him up off the street and he'd been compliant with my colleagues who helped him bathe and change into fresh clothes. He was keeping himself to himself on the ward too, not making any waves with other patients or staff. This compliant behaviour continued day after day, but so too did the uneasy feeling I had whenever I encountered him.

He stayed with us for a total of six months, during which time he spent most of his days wandering slowly and aimlessly around the unit and drifting in and out of the TV lounge. Nobody ever visited him and he never accepted our offers of a phone to use. Grunts and the briefest of responses remained his chosen method of communication, Warren never once engaging in a meaningful way with anybody at all. He was put on anti-psychotics like everybody else (Gary being an exception to the rule whenever he was there), but ultimately the doctors who assessed him couldn't find any evidence of a mental health diagnosis.

It didn't take long for me to discover that several of my colleagues shared my view that there was something 'not right' about Warren, though like me, nobody could articulate exactly what it was. That said, I think you develop a sixth sense when you work for a long time in mental health. Like all mental health nurses, I had learned to assimilate information about patients all the time, often at an unconscious level, and also to listen closely to the feelings in my gut. My colleagues and I instinctively practised more caution around Warren than we did with other patients, though I was also sure to treat him with the same care and compassion as all the others.

Less than a year after Warren was discharged back into the community, one of my colleagues arrived at work carrying a copy of the *Daily Mirror*.

'Look who it is,' she said.

I instantly recognised the pinched face and piercing eyes in the snatched press photograph.

Warren had stabbed a stranger to death in a shopping centre and was being detained indefinitely at one of the country's high-security psychiatric hospitals. Nowadays it's likely that instead of being discharged back into the community without being monitored, as he was, a patient like Warren would have been put on

105

a community treatment order. It's a slightly better system, as the patient must prove they are continuing their medication in the community, and they can be recalled to hospital for up to seventy-two hours and sectioned again at any time if need be. That said, there is no net in the world fine enough to stop every potential killer from slipping through it. Especially one like Warren, with a talent for keeping their true self buried deep beneath the surface, in more ways than one.

In sharp contrast to Seth, none of the other patients on Ward 14 knew Nikolajs's history. Staff would never disclose confidential information to other patients and Nikolajs's English was so limited that even if he'd wanted to talk about his past he'd have struggled to find the language. On one occasion we brought in a Latvian translator to help him communicate, but even then he was very resistant to talking about anything at all.

'Why's he here?' a new nursing assistant asked me casually one day, over the six o'clock tray. 'He's the sweetest old man I've ever met. I don't know how he puts up with sitting beside that Seth all day!'

The new recruit was only seventeen and had been in the job just a week or two, and when I told her his story her jaw hit the floor.

After arriving in the UK as a refugee, Nikolajs had lived a very solitary life, living alone and keeping himself to himself. Nevertheless he was well liked in his local community, and when he was in his early seventies the elderly woman who lived next door began taking food round to his house. Around this time Nikolajs developed a rash, and when it didn't shift he started to believe that his neighbour was slowly poisoning him with her home-cooked food. Nikolajs's response to this was to stab his kindly neighbour to death with a kitchen knife.

Nikolajs was subsequently diagnosed with paranoid delusions caused by paraphrenia, a condition that is not unusual in older people, causing paranoid delusions but without reducing the person's intellect or stripping away their personality in the way schizophrenia can do. Like Seth, Nikolajs was found to have acted with diminished responsibility and escaped a murder conviction. He was instead transferred to Ward 14 under Section 37/41 of the Mental Health Act, the court having decided that treatment on a secure ward was appropriate for a man of his advancing years.

'What if he thinks one of us is trying to poison him?' the young nursing assistant said, saucer-eyed. 'What if he tries to stab us with a knife when we give him his tea?'

They were not unreasonable questions. Despite being in his early eighties by this time, Nikolajs was still a strong, solid man. As unlikely as it seemed, he did represent an ongoing risk, or he wouldn't have been with us.

I told the nursing assistant that I personally never felt that I had to be more vigilant about my safety around Nikolajs. To me he was a very familiar face, just like Aggie, and the special bond we had formed mitigated the obvious concerns you might have expected me to have. Of course, Aggie had hit me that one time, but I didn't let that change our relationship. The nursing staff in general were far more wary around patients who were new to the ward, and who were to some extent an unknown quantity, as well as those who were prone to violence or were unpredictable. Besides, even if he wanted to, Nikolajs would have had a job getting hold of a weapon on the ward. All sharp knives were locked away, and the cutlery was counted in and out of the kitchen methodically. It was rare for anything to go missing, because if it did all the bedrooms would be pulled apart and searched from top to bottom. The items would always be found, and I think the patients had worked out that it really wasn't worth the upheaval.

The nursing assistant didn't look as reassured as I'd hoped.

'Whatever the patients have done, you have to treat them all the same way,' I said. 'And that means treating them as you'd expect someone you love to be nursed and cared for.'

I'd had that said to me many times since I was the same age as this young woman, but she was at the very start of her career and this was a new conversation. Seeing her absorb this truth and then continue to care for Nikolajs in the same kind and compassionate way she had when she first arrived was very rewarding. Watching her also nurse Seth with the same level of care was even more so.

CHAPTER 4

'I do not want it, I will not have it!'

'Can you smell that?'

Kim's eyes widened. We'd spent years working in clouds of cigarette smoke inside the hospital but a new era had dawned. It was 1990 and instead of staff and patients being allowed to smoke freely all over the hospital, in bedrooms, dining rooms and even in the kitchen, smoking was now only permitted outside. It meant the patients of Ward 14 would be let out into a small secure garden to enjoy an hourly cigarette, at least in theory. In practice there weren't always enough nurses on duty to supervise the garden, and given that nearly all of the staff were also smokers we'd often turn a blind eye to the rules and let patients have a cigarette with us, in our old smoking room. We considered it a perk of being on a locked ward (as mental health nurses still do to this day). After all, we had the keys, we were locked up together for hours on end and nobody could come onto the ward unless we let them in.

This smoke, however, was not coming from our yellow-walled 'secret' smoking room. Alarmingly, it was coming from the seclusion room, the only place where smoking had always been completely banned on the unit.

Kim and I went to investigate, and when we looked through the small observation window we saw Ralph sitting cross-legged on the floor, smiling up at us and thoroughly enjoying his fag.

'The cheeky devil!' I said, knowing there was only one explanation for this.

Ralph was such a heavy smoker that his blond hair had turned dirty yellow. He came from a wealthy family, his parents giving him an endless supply of cigarettes, and he was also the proud owner of a fancy guitar which he strummed with his orange fingers at every opportunity, singing along tunelessly.

Earlier in the day Ralph had picked a fight with our pub singer Victor.

'You think *you're* a musical artist?' Ralph had said snootily. Victor had very recently arrived on the ward for his annual spring visit. I had no idea why patients who experienced manic episodes had a habit of reappearing at the same time each year, and I am still none the wiser. But that was certainly a pattern I saw repeated again and again with many patients.

As always, from the moment he was admitted Victor had been belting out Elton John and Billy Joel classics at the top of his lungs, all day long, and through most of the night.

'What a joke!' Ralph mocked. 'You're just a common pub singer, ha! A pub singer!'

Not surprisingly, Victor took great exception to Ralph.

'Wanker!' Victor retaliated. 'Who d'you think you're talking to? I'm a seasoned performer – and *you*, young man, *you* can't even sing in tune!'

This brought an awkward smile of recognition to a lot of people's faces, staff and patients alike. Even Sally enjoyed Victor's put-down, and she was not exactly his biggest fan, on account of the fact that Victor never stopped reminding her of her drunken fall from grace. 'Remember that time you came to work pissed?' he asked her for years afterwards, and almost every time he saw her.

'I had flu, Victor,' she would reply.

'Bollocks!' he always said. 'You were pissed!'

Ralph was a troubled young man in many ways. Arrogant and entitled, he didn't seem to be capable of developing a relationship with anyone he came into contact with. It was such a shame as I felt progress could have been made if he'd only been less rude and patronising to everyone he met. As it was, he put all his energy into swaggering around the ward with his guitar, singing in his pancake-flat voice, and making it known he thought he was a cut above the rest. 'Practice makes perfect,' we'd say to him, gritting our teeth. At least if Ralph was occupied with his music he was less likely to cause trouble, which was what invariably happened when he got bored.

Ralph wasn't going to let his singing rival put him down. 'Did you say *I* can't sing in tune?' he sneered at Victor, before repeating loudly, over and over again, that he was nothing but a 'common pub singer'.

In the end Victor exploded, running down the long corridor as fast as his six-foot-tall, twenty-stone body would allow, shouting that he was going to 'kick the fuckin' door off' and leave this 'rat hole of a hospital'.

My colleague Nicola appeared as if by magic, which was something she had a knack of doing when trouble was brewing on the ward, particularly when Victor was the patient at the centre of it.

'Now, now, Victor,' she said, wagging her finger at him. 'Stop that now, and come with me, do you hear?'

Victor was only ever violent towards men – we never knew why – and as four-foot-something, six-stone Nicola looked like our least threatening member of staff we'd worked out that he would listen to her more than to anyone else. The tiny nurse never failed to get through to Victor, and as soon as she spoke to him he looked down at her meekly and stopped ranting. He then let Nicola take hold of his hand and lead him back to his bedroom. As he went, Victor snarled and spat at every male nurse he encountered along the way. I found it quite upsetting to witness Victor behaving that way. He was a kind and decent man when he wasn't experiencing a manic episode, and when he was discharged he would always apologise for everything he'd done and shake everyone's hand.

After winding up Victor, Ralph had taken himself into the lounge, where he began provoking a volatile middle-aged patient who the week before had covered himself in faeces in an attempt to avoid being restrained, something we had to do every time his medication was due as he always resisted it. 'What's that smell?'

Ralph said, sniffing the air dramatically. 'Is that you, shithead?' Not surprisingly, this brought the patient to his feet, fists pumping furiously.

A lively tussle ensued, and it was as a result of this that Ralph was restrained and placed in the seclusion room. Given the fact that he was now brazenly smoking in there, Ralph clearly had a very good idea he was going to end up in seclusion that day, because before he went looking for trouble, he'd popped his tobacco and a lighter up his backside.

On a typical day, when it was time for his hourly cigarette, Ralph would always stand at the door to the garden complaining bitterly about how inhumane it was that he couldn't smoke whenever and wherever he wanted to. I use the term 'garden' loosely. It was a miserable square of concrete with a couple of benches and picnic tables screwed to the ground and a huge bin in the middle that served as an ashtray. Buildings containing bedrooms surrounded three sides of the open-air space, and a fifteen-foot-high anti-climbing fence (one that wouldn't have looked out of place in a high-security prison) had been erected as the fourth wall. Patients entering the garden had to be accompanied by two members of staff at all times, which is why it wasn't always possible to let the smokers have their hourly fix.

One day, not longer after his cheeky stunt in seclusion, it was left to me to break the bad news to Ralph that we were short-staffed and so he wasn't allowed in the garden. Worse still, the charge nurse we had on duty that day was a pain in the backside and an anti-smoker, so there was no way anybody would be sneaking a fag in our indoor smoking room that day, either.

Ralph exploded and began kicking at the door repeatedly. 'Let me out!' he raged. 'This is an infringement of my human rights! All I want is a fucking cigarette. Let me out!'

'I'm really sorry, Ralph, but I just can't,' I said. 'We've got two nurses on special observations today and we just haven't got the staff right now.'

Ralph looked at me in desperation, slid to the floor and burst into tears.

'Please let me out, Belinda. I'm begging you.'

As a fellow smoker I did have sympathy for him. I could see how upset Ralph was, and how badly he was craving a cigarette. He was a young lad in his twenties – almost exactly the same age as me – and when he was locked on the ward smoking was his greatest pleasure in life.

'OK,' I said rashly. 'But only very quickly.'

I unlocked the heavy metal door to the garden, stepped outside with Ralph and then hastily locked the door behind us so nobody else would come out.

'Thank you,' he panted in relief, lighting his cigarette as fast as he could. 'I really appreciate this, thank you. You're a lifesaver, Belinda.'

I could see how much he meant it. Ralph hadn't even taken his first drag yet, but his tears had vanished and he already looked so much calmer and less stressed. Unfortunately, just as he was about to lift the cigarette to his lips I heard a colleague's personal attack alarm sound, giving us both a start.

Every member of staff had a personal attack alarm fastened by a leather strap onto a keychain belt, something that was added to our uniform a few years into my career. The belt meant our keys were more secure (whoever thought it was a good idea to shove them in your pocket as we used to do?) and the alarms couldn't be accidentally dropped or knocked off. To trigger them you pulled the alarm in a downward motion, setting off an extremely loud, piercing noise that sounded like a smoke alarm. You couldn't fail to hear it ringing around the ward, but even so it wasn't always obvious where the sound was coming from. It meant that whenever anybody's alarm went off, every member of staff would start racing around as if they were playing the 'hotter' and 'colder' game.

'I'm so sorry, Ralph,' I said. 'We need to go back inside, right now.'

'What?' he said desperately, sucking on his cigarette as if it were a straw, draining the last precious dregs of a drink. 'Can't I stay here and finish this?'

'No. I have to go, and I can't leave you here.'

'You can! Trust me! I'll just finish my cigarette and wait for you to come back. Where's the harm in that? Please?'

There was no time to waste, and I supposed Ralph was right. All he was going to do was stand there and smoke a cigarette. It wasn't such a big deal, and nothing distracted Ralph when he had a cigarette in his mouth.

Getting the balance right between being a carer and a controller is something all mental health nurses must be mindful of, and sometimes you just have to follow your gut. Anxious to get to my colleague, I made a snap decision.

'OK,' I said to Ralph. 'I'll be back shortly. I'll have to lock this door on you.'

'Cheers, Belinda,' he grinned.

Before anti-psychotic medication arrived in the 1950s, Victorian methods of restraint including straitjackets, bed straps and leather belts with manacles were accepted as a necessary way of controlling mentally disordered offenders. Critics said their use demoralised and brutalised staff as well as patients, increasing the violence used by nurses grappling with uncooperative patients. Still, it was only when a patient called William Scrivinger died from strangulation in 1829, after being strapped to his bed at Lincoln Asylum and left overnight without supervision, that reforms gradually started to be introduced and 'moral care' became the standard by which asylums were run. Despite this, by the end of the nineteenth century some of the old restraints were back with a vengeance, a symptom of the problem of overcrowding in asylums.

The use of padded cells was common practice at my hospital until the end of the 1950s, when the first anti-psychotic, chlorpromazine (a forerunner to clozapine), revolutionised the treatment of psychotic disorders. Seeing images of those miserable, dark cells had disturbed me when I was growing up, the thick, grey-cushioned walls conjuring creepy images of out-of-control lunatics thrashing around like caged animals. The feelings I experienced the first time I saw Ward 14's seclusion room have also stayed with me. Looking at the single thin mattress, positioned in the middle of the floor in an otherwise bare room (a concrete bed base came later), I was filled with a mixture of sorrow and trepidation. Just like the old padded cell, the seclusion room was designed to stop patients hurting themselves and others. Sometimes they were given a strong blanket, something that is still used occasionally today. These blankets are made of material that can't be destroyed in frustration or anger, and can't be ripped up to be used as a ligature.

However, both the padded cell and the seclusion room were also used as a form of punishment.

'If you don't behave we'll have no choice but to put you in seclusion,' one of the stern older nurses, Sister Brown, would threaten a patient, back when I worked on the open women's wards. She sounded more like a fearsome headmistress issuing a detention than a medical professional, and this threat could be provoked by anything from patients refusing to take their medication to deliberately causing trouble.

One day Sister Brown got very cross about a patient called Betty, who appeared to have gone missing. 'Where is she?' she demanded in her shrill voice.

'She's in seclusion, Sister Brown,' I said quietly, not wanting to embarrass my superior, as she had been the one who had ordered Betty into there hours earlier. Betty had been abusive and aggressive to anyone and everyone all day, telling people to fuck off and banging on the door of the nursery. 'You're not fit to have babies!' she shouted at the women who'd been admitted with postpartum psychosis. She also refused to get dressed, as she did most days, and Sister Brown decided she was not tolerating her 'unruly' behaviour a minute longer. A lot had happened since she put Betty in seclusion, though, and Sister Brown had completely forgotten what she'd done with her.

'Seclusion?' she replied sharply. 'Well, get her out of there – it's her turn to do the washing-up!'

If a person is detained under any section of the Mental Health Act, decisions regarding their treatment can be made without their consent, including the use of environmental, chemical or physical restraint to keep them safe and protect others. By chemical restraint we mean the giving of medication to placate and tranquillise a patient rather than to treat their condition.

Paraldehyde, developed more than a hundred years earlier, was the sedating drug of choice when I entered nursing. The thick liquid had to be administered via a glass syringe because it was so toxic. The advantage was that it worked quickly, though it left an awful, pungent smell of vinegar hanging in the air, and it wasn't easy to inject. In Rex's case, after so many years of regular injections (many given against his will) his buttocks were full of stinking abscesses that had erupted thanks to the multiple puncture wounds in his skin.

'I do not want it, I will not have it!' he'd protest wildly in his gravelly, Barry White baritone. It was the same every time he became manic and out of control, Rex kicking and screaming and making it abundantly clear he hated the drug as much as he hated 'fucking Jonathan Black'.

One day Rex covered himself from head to toe in the baby oil he needed for his dry skin, hoping that when we tried to restrain him in order to medicate him he'd be too slippery for us to get hold of. It worked up to a point, and it became a regular trick of Rex's, but however many nurses it took to hold him down, and however much baby oil stained our uniforms, he always got the medication in the end, often with a nurse sitting on top of him while the injection went in. I didn't blame Rex for making our job more difficult. He was very paranoid and was only trying to protect himself, and similarly I didn't feel bad about restraining him. He needed his medication and we always treated him with as much care and compassion as we possibly could while we got the job done. It may sound cruel to sit on him and none of us enjoyed it, but when you are dealing with extreme cases, sometimes there is no choice but to take extreme measures.

Acuphase gradually replaced paraldehyde, and 'let's Acuphase them' became a commonly heard cry on the ward whenever rapid sedation was required. 'PRN hourly' was another well-used instruction, PRN being an abbreviation of the Latin phrase *pro re nata*', meaning 'as required'. This can be applied to anything from paracetamol to rapid tranquillisation, and the power the nurse has to interpret what is required can unfortunately be open to abuse. I saw many patients not just sedated but wiped out completely – or 'stupozed', to use the medical term, the nurse in charge having decided they had given the dose that was 'required'.

'Bloody hell, he's built like a brick shithouse,' one of my male colleagues said.

He wasn't wrong. This patient, arrested by police for public disorder, was absolutely enormous and rippling with muscles. He was also extremely agitated when he arrived on the ward, and continued thrashing around, expressing paranoid delusions and shouting abuse, when the officers released him from his handcuffs and left us to it. I was one of half a dozen nurses trying, and failing, to restrain the man. Even just getting a grip on his arms and keeping him still in an upright position was proving impossible, and it was clear to us all that we needed to get this patient lying safely on the ground, in a prone position, as we call it, so we could sedate him.

It was much easier said than done. The man's arms were made of steel and his legs, planted firmly on the lino, were each wider than my waist. It felt like we had, quite literally, hit a brick wall.

'Give it to him now!' someone shouted.

It's not something we liked to do, but occasionally it was the best option for an extremely resistant patient like this. One of my female colleagues stepped forward into the melee of staff surrounding the angry man and swiftly administered the paraldehyde, straight through the leg of his trousers.

Normally a shot of sedative starts to kick in almost instantaneously, but several minutes later the patient was still as lively and out of control as ever. We were all scratching our heads, but then I realised that one of the male nurses had disappeared.

'Where's Jack?' I said.

We all looked around, and there was Jack, passed out against a wall along the corridor.

In the confusion, the nurse had mistakenly injected our colleague instead of our patient.

It was not the first memorable restraint story of my career, and it would certainly not be the last.

'Jason needs his meds. Come on, let's work out who's doing what.'

It was a Tuesday morning and I was lacking in sleep and energy after a good night out at Benny's. I nodded, though I was not relishing the thought of having to wrestle with this patient, who was another six-foot-tall hulk of a man.

Jason was a former boxer who frequently arrived at the hospital in a Black Maria, having been handcuffed and dragged off the streets by a bunch of burly police officers because of his manic behaviour. This included running around the streets at all hours of the day and night, punching his fists as if in training for a boxing match.

Giving him his regular medication – in his case the slow-release depot injection in his buttock – always proved a trial. Jason was a force to be reckoned with, the fact that it sometimes took ten officers to restrain him and bring him onto the ward telling you all you need to know.

When Jason was experiencing a manic episode he would refuse to eat and drink and spent all day exercising by running on the spot, boxing invisible opponents and doing push-ups around the ward.

'I'm not having it,' he would bellow when it was time for his injection.

Before we got to know him better we tried the gentle approach, saying, 'Come on, Jason, let's do this the easy way,' but he never responded well to this and would bat us away like flies.

I felt sorry for Jason. Even for a giant of a man like him, having a depot injection was a very painful and uncomfortable experience. For a former boxer, and a man who remained proud of his strength and physical prowess, being restrained and injected in the backside must have been a particularly undignified experience, not least because we'd come to accept that the only way to get the job done was to ambush Jason en masse.

I sat down with five colleagues in the lounge to decide who was taking which limb, who would hold Jason's head still, and which nurse would pull down his pants and inject the depot.

'Right, are we all ready?' one of the male nurses said, getting to his feet. 'Here comes Rocky. Let's go for it.'

I turned around to see a very intense-looking Jason in the corridor, jogging towards us.

'Ready as I'll ever be,' I thought, taking a deep breath.

Just at that moment Chris, a male nurse, appeared from nowhere, charging towards Jason at lightning speed. The rest of us watched agog as he leapt in the air and launched himself at Jason's neck. We all knew Chris was fit – he spent all of his spare time rock climbing – but he was the smallest male nurse on the unit and so slim he looked like wind would blow him over. Nobody could have imagined he had the strength to tackle Jason alone, but how wrong we were.

Jason was toppled like a stone statue, crashing to the ground in one fell swoop, whereupon Chris sat firmly on his chest to keep him trapped to the floor.

'Where on earth did that come from?' someone asked.

'I don't know,' another colleague replied. 'But he's saved us a job – let's finish it, quick!'

Jason never complained about the unorthodox restraint, or the fact that he had his injection given to him in sight of other patients sitting in the lounge and walking along the corridor. As I've said before, a textbook restraint was virtually unheard of, and as for the lack of privacy, giving injections in communal areas was commonplace. The need to medicate trumped everything, though this would never happen today, the risk to the patient being unacceptable.

Once his meds had kicked in and he was no longer manic Jason was very fond of us all, and in particular Neil, our calm and friendly charge nurse.

'What's that nutter playing at?' Jason yelled one day, fists clenched as he stared angrily at Stuart, a small, weak patient who had recently arrived from a top-security hospital. Stuart had derailed a train by throwing two concrete blocks off a railway bridge, convinced he was James Bond and that the train was full of spies. He'd spent more than twenty years locked up alongside some of the country's most notorious offenders before coming to us when his physical health declined and it was decided he no longer needed the very highest level of secure care.

Like so many patients, Stuart had no insight whatsoever into his mental health. None of us had managed to establish any kind of therapeutic relationship with him and he was also completely unresponsive to any form of psychological therapy or medication. Today he had taken it upon himself to attack our charge nurse at every opportunity, launching himself at Neil and trying to strangle him. As soon as another member of staff went over to intervene, Stuart stopped what he was doing and calmly walked away. This went on for hours, Stuart randomly bursting through doors and appearing around corners before throwing himself at Neil. The rest of us found it quite amusing, and as Neil was so laid-back (and wasn't actually being hurt) he just kept taking it.

Jason, however, was far less tolerant. He couldn't stand his favourite member of staff being treated like this and was getting increasingly angry about Stuart's behaviour.

'What's he doing?' he called out repeatedly. 'He's a nutter, what's he playing at?'

We told Jason not to worry. We had this under control, and he was not to get involved. Did he listen? Did he heck! I came out of the dining room after the six o'clock tray to find Jason standing on Stuart's throat and Neil desperately trying to restrain Jason all by himself.

'I'm sorry, I'm sorry,' Stuart was saying, struggling to breathe and gasping for air under the weight of Jason's size-twelve slipper.

Several other nurses arrived on the scene. 'You go home,' we told Neil. 'We can handle this.'

It was an unusual situation for a group of nurses to be telling our charge nurse what to do but Neil agreed, knowing that once he was out of the picture the situation would ease, as it immediately did.

'Neil is perfectly safe,' we told Jason, who let us lead him away from Stuart as soon as Neil had left the unit. 'We're afraid Stuart was very ill today, but it's all OK now.'

With both Neil and Jason out of the way Stuart also calmed down, and before I left for the evening I saw him sitting quietly in the lounge, engrossed in a film. I was pleased to be able to write in the night log that the ward was perfectly calm at the end of my shift. 'All's well that ends well,' I thought.

It wasn't until I turned to leave the lounge that I noticed what Stuart was gripped by on the TV – it was an old 1960s James Bond movie starring Sean Connery.

Ash was another fairly regular visitor to Ward 14. A man in his forties with a significant stammer, he would typically be brought in by the police on a Section 136 order, having been found in a state of drug-induced psychosis on the streets, full of amphetamines and Carlsberg Special Brew. Back then it was a question of nursing Ash on the ward while the drugs left his system and giving him sedatives and anti-psychotic medication. One day he was more paranoid than usual, and aggressive with it, trying to assault the staff and being rude and verbally abusive. The charge nurse decided the safest place for Ash was in the seclusion room, where he should be observed every six minutes until he was calm enough to be let out.

I was one of the team of nurses on duty and we carried out the observations exactly as instructed. However, the last time we checked him it was immediately obvious something was wrong. Ash was facing the back wall and was very calm and quiet, and as he slowly turned around to face us we saw that he had blood streaming down his face from his left eye. For a moment, the shock caused us all to stand stock still. Ash's eyeball was missing, the dreadful realisation mobilising us all into action. While one of my colleagues provided first aid and two others searched the seclusion room and Ash himself for the eyeball, I phoned for the emergency doctor.

We couldn't find the eyeball and Ash was saying nothing as he was rushed to A & E. Eventually, he told the horrified doctors what had happened to his eye.

'It's in my s-s-s-stomach,' he said.

'What do you mean?'

'I've e-e-e-eaten it.'

Ash subsequently had his eye socket stitched up, insisting he would never wear a false eye, and when he returned to the ward the following year he was proudly sporting a red eyepatch, a nod to Manchester United, his favourite football team.

Sidney was a lovely Irish patient with a twinkle in his eye, and as a student Jonathan had the pleasure of looking after him on an open ward at the hospital. Sidney was a broad, hefty man, standing six foot four inches tall and strong with it, in mind as well as body.

'I'm leaving,' he announced one day, striding purposefully towards the unsecured door with Jonathan and another student nurse in hot pursuit.

'You can't,' Jonathan implored. 'You need to stay here.'

Sidney wasn't listening, and so Jonathan and his colleague each lunged forward and grabbed hold of an arm as tightly as they could. It was a valiant attempt to keep their patient on the ward, but given that their combined weight was probably less than Sidney's twenty-something stone, he was completely undaunted. Just as Agatha had the power to do, Sidney raised his arms out to the sides of his body, lifting the two young men clean off the floor, their legs dangling as he carried on heading to the exit.

In the end it took six staff members to keep him on the ward, and from then on whenever Sidney threatened to leave (which he did frequently), every available member of staff would spring into action straight away, ambushing him from all angles. Even so, Sidney would usually manage to shake off even the biggest and strongest male nurses without too much trouble.

After countless battles, the sister decided to try a different tactic.

'We've taken Sidney's clothes away,' she told the staff. 'He's going to have to make do with his pyjamas and dressing gown, then he can't go anywhere.'

How wrong she was. I'll never forget Jonathan relaying what happened next. Determined not to be beaten, Sidney stole a flowery Crimplene dress from one of the older ladies on the ward. Given his size, it was like a top on him, and it didn't exactly go with his paisley-patterned pyjama bottoms either. Nevertheless, Sidney had the gall and gumption to escape from the hospital in his make-shift outfit. Audaciously, he then caught a bus to town, went to the station and took a train to Liverpool, where he hit the town for a wild night out.

'Is he back?' I asked, amused and aghast in equal measure. 'Is he OK?'

'Yes,' Jonathan chuckled. 'When he'd had enough he went to a local convent and asked the nuns to return him to us. I don't think he'll be going anywhere for a while. He says he's shattered.'

Very early on in my career, I saw a unit manager responding to a patient who had set off a fire alarm, was out of control and needed to be restrained. I watched in horror as the manager ran down the corridor, two pool balls clenched very visibly in his fists. When the patient saw them he knew exactly what this meant and held his hands in the air, as if in surrender.

'Good,' the manager said. 'I won't be needing these now.'

Thankfully, I never saw anything like that again. The vast

majority of nurses I have worked with have wanted to care for people with dignity and compassion.

One day my colleague Roy went into the male dormitory to open the windows and give the room a general check over once all the patients were up and about and installed on the rest of the ward. Nobody followed him down the corridor because we all believed the dorm was empty, but when Roy entered the room a patient who was in for assessment leapt up from the shadows, punched him in the face and grabbed him in a stranglehold. This was in the days before we carried personal attack alarms and when our keys were floating around in our pockets. It was also in an era when the practice of restraining a patient was known as 'control and restraint' as opposed to 'care and responsibility', and it was many years before 'breakaway techniques' were taught, training nurses how to protect themselves as well as the patient during a restraint.

Feeling himself passing out, Roy took drastic action, somehow managing to free himself in such a way that he was able to punch the patient in the face several times. Not a 'breakaway technique' that would ever be taught in a classroom, but it quite possibly saved Roy's life and was certainly never called into question by the charge nurse on duty.

Abuses of many kinds have plagued mental health care for more than a century, and there's extensive documented evidence of it through the years, largely thanks to journalists and whistle-blowers. The 1887 book *Ten Days in a Mad-House* was written by

American journalist Nellie Bly, who famously feigned insanity to be committed to an asylum in Manhattan, exposing a regime of brutality and neglect, including patients being roughly washed and scrubbed and forced to share towels with others who had boils and open sores.

Nellie Bly's exposé caused a scandal, but it didn't stop abuse in asylums. Fast-forward to 1967 and Barbara Robb, a psychotherapist and campaigner for improved care for the elderly in long-stay wards, published *Sans Everything*, highlighting inadequate and inhumane treatment in seven NHS hospitals. The title referred to the fact the patients lost their privacy and dignity and had all personal possessions stripped from them, including dentures, hearing aids and spectacles. Other abuses included patients being roughly handled, sworn at, teased and slapped, and staff running a production-line system of bathing.

'The sufferers might be *your* parents, your friends or relatives; might even be you in a few years' time,' Barbara Robb wrote. 'This problem cries to heaven for attention.'

More than fifty years have passed since Barbara Robb published those words, yet patients are still suffering dreadfully in mental health settings

The long-overdue 'Seni's Law' sets out measures to reduce the inappropriate use of force in mental health units. Named in memory of Olaseni Lewis, twenty-three, who died in 2010 after being restrained by eleven police officers while he was a vulnerable, voluntary patient at Bethlem Royal Hospital in London, Seni's

Law finally came into force in March 2022. It is much-needed, sadly. Though deaths are rare, the problem of inappropriate use and overuse of restraint continues, as a 2022 Care Quality Commission review showed.

In recent years the physical as well as psychological abuse of vulnerable patients has been exposed by undercover investigations at several institutions. Footage filmed in 2011 at Winterbourne View, a private hospital in South Gloucestershire, showed staff repeatedly assaulting and harshly restraining disabled patients under chairs. In 2019 at Whorlton Hall in County Durham – a privately run, NHS-funded unit – staff admitted to an undercover reporter that they deliberately hurt, threatened and intimidated patients, while in 2022 at the Edenfield Centre, a secure NHS mental health hospital in Greater Manchester, staff were found verbally abusing patients about their weight and bodily functions, and one patient had been held in seclusion for over a year.

Where a culture of abuse develops, there is generally an underlying lack of training, supervision and support for staff as well as a rapid staff turnover, staff working long hours, high numbers of agency staff coming in and a distinct lack of clinical leadership.

Nowadays the managers predominantly work Monday to Friday from nine to five, whereas in my day sisters and charge nurses worked shifts alongside the rest of us, including nights. The nursing officers (the equivalent of matrons in general nursing) also worked across all the shifts. It meant there was the constant presence of senior, experienced nurses who provided clinical leadership, and in addition to this qualified nurses always outnumbered unqualified nurses. We would typically have four or five qualified nurses and one or two nursing assistants or support workers per shift, which is the opposite of what happens today, both privately and in the NHS. It is difficult to compute how we have managed to go backwards in this regard, despite decades of reform designed to improve patient care.

Ernie was in his early seventies when I first met him in 1988. I was in my early twenties then and was astonished to learn that he had been admitted to the old asylum when he was around my age or younger. It meant he had arrived before the start of the Second World War, and possibly when George V was still on the throne.

Diagnosed with paranoid schizophrenia, Ernie had become well known throughout the hospital for being extremely violent, and in common with some of the other long-standing patients, he had a telltale dent on the side of his head. I don't know exactly when or why the decision was taken to lobotomise Ernie, or exactly why he had been admitted to the hospital in the first place. Lobotomising patients was supposed to be a last resort when all else failed, but there are suspicions that the old asylums carried out the procedure too liberally, as a way of controlling disruptive patients in an overcrowded setting, exactly in the way Jack Nicholson's character was mistreated in One Flew Over the Cuckoo's Nest. A very small percentage of lobotomised patients stayed the same or were slightly improved, but like Nicholson's Randle McMurphy, the majority suffered life-changing, negative effects to their personality and behaviour.

For Ernie, the lobotomy had been catastrophic. The only word in his vocabulary was 'yumyo', and Ernie had also been robbed of the ability to wash or dress himself, go to the toilet, feed himself or even have a drink without assistance. He would be brought onto Ward 14 from one of the male long-stay wards whenever he was going through a particularly bad phase and his violent behaviour was out of control. He was inevitably in a bad mood when he arrived, which meant he walked around everywhere very quickly, punching walls, sending chairs flying and muttering 'yumyo'. This could go on for days.

Ernie always had his favourite nurses on our ward, and I'm happy to say I was one of them, which meant that when he was eventually in a better mood, he'd allow me to hold his hand and walk up and down the ward with him. I loved Ernie dearly, and it's fair to say many people had a huge soft spot for him. His violent behaviour was tolerated and accepted by patients and staff alike, and even the regular visitors to the ward were adept at jumping out of the way when they saw him pacing towards them, punching a wall or throwing a chair. The only person who never showed compassion was Seth, who used to shout out horrible things whenever he saw Ernie. 'What's that idiot doing?' he'd yell. 'He's not reet in the head.' Meeting Ernie made me want to learn more about lobotomies, and I was horrified by what I found. It was in 1935 that the Portuguese neurologist Egas Moniz learned of an experiment in which the frontal lobes of two chimpanzees were removed, resulting in less violent behaviour and making them more compliant. Moniz decided to repeat the experiment with humans, by drilling through the skulls of unsuspecting patients suffering from mental health diagnoses and cutting into their frontal lobes. Afterwards he published a paper proclaiming lobotomy as an innovative way to treat such illnesses as schizophrenia and psychosis, and subsequently a physician called Walter Freeman helped popularise lobotomies in America. With no surgical training, Freeman decided that instead of drilling holes into the sides of the skull, he would stab into the patient's brain with an ice pick inserted through the eye socket. He allegedly perfected this method to the point where it only took him twelve minutes to perform the procedure, which he did in his travelling van, the unsterilised 'Lobotomobile'. Sixteen years after Moniz published his paper the first anti-psychotic medication appeared at Sainte-Anne Hospital, a psychiatric hospital in Paris, drastically reducing the number of surgical lobotomies around the world. Nevertheless, thousands of patients were lobotomised in the decades that followed and modifications of the neurosurgery were still being carried out in the UK until as recently as 2010. To this day, the procedure remains one of the most criticised and controversial in medical history.

Ernie never left the grounds, but we would accompany him to some of the social events held in the hospital, like dances in the ballroom and sports events in the gardens in the summer. I don't know whether he enjoyed these outings or not. I would search his face for any signs, but I never found any. One of the very few photographs I have from my days on Ward 14 shows me with our wonderful Ernie, giving him a look of love as he stares blankly into space.

I was too immature to question the system I found myself entrenched in as a very young woman, though by today's standards many practices at the hospital were dubious, and would certainly not reach the benchmark for 'best nursing practice' in this day and age.

When my mother worked on the hospital's geriatric ward, patient numbers were high, staffing numbers low and there were not enough hands or hours in the day to care for patients with the dignity they deserved. One of her regular tasks was to assist the patients who couldn't feed themselves. Those men and women were known as 'feeders', and my mother would sit up to eight patients in a semicircle with a bowl of brown, sludgy liquidised food in front of each of them. She would then walk from one to the other, putting a spoonful of food in each patient's mouth until the bowls were empty.

I would take part in a similarly undignified practice when I was seventeen and working on Sister Kane's long-term women's ward. One of my jobs was to towel dry about fifty patients in a row and put them in V-necked, hospital-issue long-sleeved night-dresses. Two other nurses were part of this production line, one undressing the patients and the other washing them down with a wet flannel, all in front of each other and under the stark glare of a fluorescent strip light. None of the patients had their own clothes or toiletries, let alone any comfort or privacy. The towels were thin and scratchy, the floor of the bathroom was made of pale-blue lino that looked and felt as cold as stone, and the white wall tiles were stained and grimy after years and years of use. It saddens me, looking back; it was a system not dissimilar to the one Barbara Robb had criticised in mental institutions decades earlier.

I was taught that if a patient was non-compliant, for instance by not holding out their arm when you needed to give them an injection, you could nip them in a fleshy part of their body. 'Administering a short shock is likely to encourage the patient to comply,' I was instructed by a senior nurse. 'And an appropriate nip will not cause any permanent damage.'

I naively did as I was told, gently giving the most difficult patients a little squeeze in the loose skin on the underside of their upper arms. I shudder at the memory of it now. Thankfully the practice was stopped at the hospital while I was still in the early stages of my career, although only after one of our male patients was found to have scores of nip marks under his arms.

Back in the day, we tittered about Sister Brown taking Betty out of isolation to do the washing-up, and putting her back in afterwards, but with the benefit of hindsight and many years of experience I see this in a very different light now. It should never have happened. Even making milky tea with three sugars in the giant teapot, and serving it up to every patient whether they liked it or not, was an unacceptable practice.

Sometimes, I tried to make little improvements. The 'bundles' of clothing worn by the men on my first ward had to be put together in the laundry room, day bundles being made up by the night nurses and night bundles by the day nurses. The night staff would take a shirt, a jumper and a pair of trousers from separate piles and roll them into a bundle for each patient, and the day nurses rolled up a pyjama top and a pair of pyjama bottoms ready for the night staff. There was no size or colour coordination. Some of the clothes were bought with the patients' own money, others provided by the hospital and some were donations, and it was common to see patients with half-mast trousers and sleeves down to their knees or vice versa.

'This is sad,' I thought. 'I need to sort this out.'

I worked days then and so I could only influence pyjamas, but at least that was a start, I reasoned. I saw my chance one quiet Sunday afternoon, when I paired up piles and piles of pyjamas into matching colours and sizes and made three new signs that said 'Small pairs', 'Medium pairs' and 'Large pairs'. I was delighted with myself.

At changeover the next day the charge nurse, a quietly spoken man, asked who had made the new signs in the laundry. This was my chance to shine. 'Me!' I beamed. 'It was me!' With that he grabbed me by the arm and dragged me down the long corridor.

'What does that sign say?' he demanded.

'Small pairs, medium pairs,' I started, reading my own signs.

'Not those, those!' he said pointing at the old ones that said simply 'tops' and 'bottoms'.

'Tops and bottoms,' I said, my face starting to redden.

He huffed and puffed as he ripped my new signs off the wall, then told me to put everything back the way I found it.

It wasn't the last time I'd get into trouble for trying to treat the patients a little more kindly. Letting Ralph smoke in the garden was another such example. During the first few years of my career, patients throughout the hospital had the right to smoke anywhere between the hours of 6 a.m. and 10 p.m. They weren't allowed to have matches or lighters, which was understandable, but most could keep hold of their own cigarettes. However, some patients weren't trusted with their cigarettes and were only given one, on the hour, the last one being dished out at 10 p.m. Some would have chain-smoked their way through a whole packet until it was empty, it was argued, while other patients recognised all too well what a prized commodity cigarettes were, notably female patients from the open wards who offered sex in return for a packet of cigs, or even for just a couple of cigs, depending on how desperate they were. This happened well away from the nursing staff, typically in the woods or the hospital grounds, and was something we had no control over. The male patients never spoke about it but one of the female patients had a habit of spilling the beans. 'I shagged him, Belinda, for a packet of fags,' she would say, or, 'I let him touch me for a fag.'

Despite this, I never liked withholding cigarettes from patients. As a smoker myself I understood how important it was to have a puff on a cigarette, something that worked to Ralph's advantage. Research in recent years has concluded that nicotine may temporarily reduce some symptoms of schizophrenia, hence why smoking is more prevalent amongst this group of people. Perhaps if we'd known that then, the rules would not have been quite so punitive, and I would not have ended up leaving Ralph locked out in the garden.

'Where's Ralph?' a cleaner asked.

Fuck, fuck, fuck.

'I'll have a look around for him,' I replied innocently.

It was a full three hours since I'd let Ralph into the garden to have his cigarette and, after running around the ward towards the screeching noise of the panic alarm and then helping my colleague with whatever the emergency was, I'd forgotten all about him.

I ran to the garden as fast as my legs would carry me. Even though it was springtime the weather was miserable that day, and I was hoping that the fact Ralph had had three hours to chain-smoke his way through a packet of fags would make up for him being left outside for so long in the cold, damp air.

I unlocked the heavy door, flung it open and then stood there and stared, exactly like I did the day when my car was stolen and I looked at the empty spot, not quite believing what I was seeing. Or not seeing.

Shit, shit, shit.

I ran back to the ward and found Jonathan.

'Shit, shit, shit,' I said.

'Just go and tell Neil,' he said. 'He'll handle it, don't worry.'

I'd developed such a good relationship with our lovely charge nurse that he would give me ciggies at the end of the month when I couldn't afford to buy any until payday. As I'd seen with Sally's slip-up, he was a fair and forgiving man, although I had to acknowledge that this was a rather more serious situation.

I sloped off to Neil's office, heart in my mouth.

'For fuck's sake, Belinda,' he said.

Neil couldn't quite believe my stupidity when I explained exactly what I'd done. His incredulity was written all over his face, but all he did was send me off with a warning that I must learn from this mistake and never repeat it. Nowadays I would be suspended and ultimately sacked for making such a major error. As innocent and naive as it was, this was a secure ward and I'd breached the carefully thought-out procedures it was my job to follow.

In his daily report Neil simply noted: 'Ralph was in the garden having a cigarette when Staff Nurse Gibson's attention was distracted and Ralph must have climbed over the fence and escaped.'

The missing patient procedure was implemented and that was the end of it. All the staff knew what had happened, and probably most of the patients too, but to my relief and amazement Neil's brief but generously worded sentence wasn't questioned by anybody. Nevertheless, every day I arrived at work feeling sick to my stomach, discreetly asking my colleagues, 'Has Ralph been found?'

Day after day, the answer was no. To my shame and despair, our yellow-haired, orange-fingered patient seemed to have disappeared without trace. 'Good riddance!' Victor said one day, realising Ralph had gone but not questioning why his guitar was still by his bed.

Like the majority of patients on the ward, Ralph had been admitted to the hospital under Section 3 of the Mental Health Act, applied by two doctors and an approved mental health professional. In Ralph's case it was his social worker who agreed that he had a mental health diagnosis, one he was unwilling to accept needed to be treated in hospital. A Section 3 order is initially applied for six months, then another six months if needed and then annually for as long as necessary, which in many secure units is years and years. Treatment can be forced on you if you refuse medication, and this was true of Ralph, who was diagnosed with paranoid schizophrenia, refused to take oral medication and always had to be restrained to be given a depot injection. His resistance was understandable, given that he genuinely thought there was nothing wrong with him.

Having said all of that, if you are under a Section 3 order and you can survive in the community for twenty-eight days without incident, you are deemed to be no longer in need of detention and are therefore released from your section. It's a little-known fact, but one I was about to become very well acquainted with.

I was on a day off when Jonathan phoned to tell me that Ralph had returned to the ward to gloat about the fact he had managed to go missing for twenty-eight days. 'You have to remove me off my section,' he announced, pompously explaining the technicalities of a Section 3 order. It was an odd thing to do, given that if he'd simply stayed in the community the section would have automatically lapsed, but Ralph was the type of person who took great pleasure in rubbing salt in another person's wounds, and he wasn't going to deny himself the joy of telling us to our faces that he was the winner in this situation.

'You'll see him tomorrow,' Jonathan then told me. 'He's got his guitar back and he's still singing tunelessly, by the way.'

'What?'

I was confused, and Jonathan couldn't stop laughing when he told me the punchline to the story. It turned out Ralph wasn't as clever as he thought he was. He'd miscalculated, and when he arrived back on the ward it was in fact only twenty-seven days since his escape, so he was promptly locked up again.

When I was next on duty Neil caught my eye and then looked over at Ralph, who was unhappily sandwiched between Agatha and Seth at the dining table. 'Here,' Neil said, handing me a couple of fags and giving me a smile.

It was two days until payday, a payday I would be very relieved to reach. I couldn't wait for my break, and when I enjoyed those two cigarettes later that day, I sat cross-legged and smiling on the floor, in tribute to Ralph and his terrible maths skills.

CHAPTER 5

'Why are you doing this to yourself?'

'What happened to her?' I asked, curious to know why the rosy-cheeked young woman in the side room was confined to bed by a large and very unusual plaster cast. We weren't in the habit of nursing patients with broken bones but even if this girl had been on a general rather than a locked mental health ward I'd have been intrigued, because I'd never seen a cast like this one. The thick plaster of Paris structure extended from just under Michelle's breastbone to the bottom of her hips, encasing her stomach in the most unusual barrel-shaped form.

'She's only here for a couple of days, before we transfer her to a unit that specialises in self-harm,' one of my colleagues explained at the start of my shift. This older nurse was fairly new to the hospital and didn't know I'd been working on Ward 14 for several years. 'Have you had any experience of self-harm?' she asked.

'Yes, but nothing like this, I don't think,' I replied, already morbidly fascinated by what I was about to hear.

Michelle was a very persistent self-harmer, well-practised in digging her nails and any sharp objects she could find into her stomach, clawing away so zealously that she broke the skin and kept delving deeper and deeper. She had been cleaned up, stitched up and bandaged on multiple occasions, but she would always try to rip off the bandages, often under her bedclothes in the middle of the night. Sometimes she fought so hard with the nurses who tried to restrain her that they had to sit on her arms and legs until she calmed down. Michelle's care team had decided that putting her in plaster was the only way to protect her from herself, and she was placed on three-to-one observations to make sure she didn't try to claw underneath the plaster, or start excavating a different part of her body.

When it was my turn to sit in with her, along with two other nurses, Michelle was being visited by her parents and slightly younger sister. They appeared to be a very kind and supportive family, though I say 'appeared' because, as I've said before, all too often we would find out that there had been a history of abuse. Unfortunately, I'd found this to be true of patients across the board, regardless of their diagnosis.

Michelle was a pleasant, pretty girl, aged nineteen, and she was smiling and chatting away quite happily to everyone in the room. It was December, and a newspaper her dad brought in had a 'year in review' feature across the centre pages. 1987 had been quite a year, marked by several disasters including the sinking of the MS *Herald of Free Enterprise* ferry in Zeebrugge, the Hungerford massacre, the 'Great Storm' and the King's Cross fire. 'They forgot the biggest disaster of all,' Michelle said, pointing out that Margaret Thatcher had secured her third term in office that summer. Everybody laughed, Michelle the loudest, but it was a disconcerting scene. It wasn't just that the girl taking centre stage was encased in plaster. Whatever she said and however big a smile she had on her face, I always felt a deep aura of sadness surrounding Michelle. She was only on the ward for a very short time but I've never forgotten her, or what she taught me about the lengths some lost souls go to when they need to expunge their distress.

The Adult Psychiatric Morbidity Survey (2014) reported that in England the proportion of people aged sixteen to seventy-four years who reported having ever self-harmed increased from 2.4 per cent in 2000, to 3.8 per cent in 2007, to 6.4 per cent in 2014. This increase was observed in both men and women and across age groups, and the figures are probably an underestimate as many cases go unreported. In contrast to suicidal or parasuicidal behaviour, self-harm is a way of managing or coping with overwhelming or distressing thoughts and experiences. It can manifest itself in varying degrees, and it was those men and women who practised extreme self-harm who ended up on Ward 14. Sometimes they had also committed offences or had other mental health issues, but in the main this group of patients were admitted to us because other mental health wards were not able to manage their behaviour.

Quite often the patients would be young women with a diagnosis of borderline personality disorder, frequently with a history of neglect and sexual abuse. I learned early on that women tended to self-harm by cutting their arms and legs, whereas men were more likely to hit themselves, or burn their skin. This pattern continues today, though as the years have passed we've become more sophisticated in how we work with people who self-harm. For instance, we make sure patients can clean their own wounds if they choose, and we encourage them to tell us what they have done so we can ensure they receive the proper care. While knives and other sharp objects are locked away, we have accepted that we can't eliminate absolutely everything a person could harm themselves with, because where there is an absolute, overwhelming need for a patient to self-harm, they will find a way. This approach, combined with psychotherapy, gives better outcomes for the patients, and though self-harm is still present on mental health wards, I've seen a reduction in the escalating levels of self-harm, and in the extremes of injuries suffered.

The stories of four other patients have also stayed imprinted on my mind, so extreme, unusual and alarming were their acts of self-harm.

'Here's your tea,' I said brightly to the elderly Chinese gentleman.

'I can't drink that,' said Mr Lee. 'I have no throat.'

'Yes, you can. Look, you do have a throat, it's just like mine.'

I took a drink of tea from one of the blue plastic mugs laid out in the dining room, pointing to my throat as I drank it. Then I pointed to his throat and told him he could take a drink from his mug and swallow it exactly as I just had.

'OK,' he said, looking at me suspiciously.

With that Mr Lee began to lift his right arm very slowly, reaching towards the tea.

Success!

Unfortunately, this wasn't the case. Mr Lee changed his mind a moment later, letting his arm drop like a lead weight into his lap. 'Ah, I can't hold the cup, I have no hands.'

Mr Lee had nihilistic delusions, a condition that in his case meant he thought parts of his body were missing. Other patients experiencing nihilistic delusions – also known as *délires de néga-tion* – believe they are dead, decomposed or annihilated, having lost their internal organs. I was very young when I encountered Mr Lee, on one of the open male wards, and the concept both intrigued and appalled me. I felt very sorry for him, and when I moved to work on another ward I was keen to keep tabs on him.

'How is Mr Lee?' I asked another of the nursing assistants. 'He was such a nice man.'

'Oh,' my friend said. 'Not a good ending. Or perhaps that's not the best way to put it!'

Me Lee had been discharged home, she explained, and when he was alone in his flat he chopped off his penis with a penknife.

'It was one of those Swiss Army ones, like they sell on the market,' she explained, unable to stop herself from giggling. 'I'm so sorry, what am I like?'

I laughed too. It was either that or cry, and even though we were a pair of naive teenagers we knew very well that we didn't really find this story funny – quite the opposite. As inappropriate as our exchange was on the surface, we relied on black humour to keep us going at times like this. As I've said before, it was an essential tool of the trade, though some patients' stories were so horrific there were moments when our go-to secret weapon evaded us.

The police escorted sixteen-year-old Emmanuel onto Ward 14 after neighbours reported hearing strange noises coming from his house while his parents were away. When the officers went to investigate they found Emmanuel in a deeply traumatised state and the interior of the house dismantled around him. Desperate to find the source of the voices that were taunting and threatening him, Emmanuel had pulled the radiators and even the plasterboard off the walls, stripping them back to the brick in some rooms and pulling out pipework in order to discover where his tormentors were hiding.

'I have to find them,' he told the police. 'They have to be stopped before they kill me.'

It emerged that his parents had gone to Spain two weeks earlier, leaving Emmanuel home alone. He had absolutely no insight into his mental health, and what he must have gone through for all of that time, utterly terrified and isolated, was dreadful to imagine.

Emmanuel's history revealed that he'd been admitted to an acute mental health unit the previous year after being talked down from throwing himself off a motorway bridge. He had also overdosed on painkillers on more than one occasion.

The psychiatrist swiftly diagnosed him with paranoid schizophrenia and he began to have regular sessions with our psychologist, at the time a very competent and empathetic woman who was also clearly very moved by Emmanuel's story. He was compliant with his medication and making good progress in all areas, and very soon the psychologist was pushing for him to move into supported accommodation in a special unit for young people. I was fully in favour of this, as were all of the nurses on the ward. This boy needed the very best specialist care we could find.

It was the middle of the summer and I went on holiday to Greece with another student nurse, staying in a ropey hostel, where we were dismayed at not being able to flush away our toilet paper. On the morning of my return to work I walked into the small lounge to find a group of my colleagues sitting in stunned silence, the log from the previous night laid out before them.

'What is it?' I asked, already knowing this was going to be something very hard to hear.

Nobody wanted to say it out loud and one of my colleagues pushed the log towards me. 'It's awful, Belinda.'

When I read it I felt like dropping to my knees.

Emmanuel had taken a razor blade to his lips and tried to cut them off, mutilating himself in the most appalling manner. The nurse who found him described the scene as 'like something out of *Hammer House of Horror*', Emmanuel so drenched in blood it looked as if he was dressed in red pyjamas, his face having been mauled by a wild animal.

It took some time for the devastating backstory to do the rounds on the ward, and when it did it was met with unanimous, unfiltered shock and disbelief. It emerged that in his sessions with the psychologist, Emmanuel disclosed that he had been sexually abused for years by his controlling, violent father, and that his father frequently made him give his mother oral sex, while he looked on.

Emmanuel was rushed to the general hospital for emergency surgery, and in the days that followed a string of emergency multidisciplinary team meetings were held, involving the police and social services. I never saw him again. After he'd recovered from his facial surgery he was moved directly into the supported facility the psychologist and other members of his care team arranged for him. We heard that he was refusing to press charges against either of his parents. His mother never resurfaced after her trip to Spain and as far as we knew his father, a well-known local hard man, continued with his life uninterrupted.

When I saw the size of Sam's file my heart sank. Most patients arrived with some history already written down, and then a doctor or nurse would fill in a lengthy admission document detailing everything from their forensic history to past admissions and risk assessments. Added to this were the results of a physical assessment and any information provided by other agencies, such as social services, the police or the probation service. Everything was written by hand and most patients' files were pretty hefty, but Sam's was a particularly huge tome. It would take an age to sift through that lot, I thought.

'Twenty years old, history of self-harm and parasuicidal behaviour,' my colleague Gayle said, as observant and helpful as ever as she popped her head round the door. 'Admitted from A & E following a paracetamol overdose, the latest in a long line.'

The ward was extremely busy and Gayle continued on her way to take over some observations. 'Thanks,' I said, looking at my watch and thinking I could spare at least five minutes to have a look through the file.

Sam had caught my attention when I saw him in the lounge that morning. He was wearing a pair of dungarees and a baggy black beret over his curly hair. If it wasn't for the fact he had red hair and a pale face dotted with freckles, he'd have looked just like the lead singer from Dexys Midnight Runners. Though it wasn't just Sam's appearance that made him stand out; his personality did that too.

'Morning!' I said, casting my eye around the room as I always did.

'Good morning,' he said politely, looking up from his game of clock patience.

There were many occasions when I received nothing but a grunt in reply to my morning greeting, even when the lounge was filled with very familiar faces, which it nearly always was. Sam seemed like a lovely boy, I thought, but before I had the chance to engage him in any kind of conversation a kerfuffle broke out down the corridor, diverting my attention.

'I'm ever so sorry, Vicar,' I could hear the sister saying while a patient was being noisily restrained, by the sound of it. 'I can't apologise enough.'

I shot out of the lounge to see if I was needed, unable to hide the smirk on my face as I registered the acute embarrassment in the sister's voice. I wasn't a fan of this particular sister, Judy, to put it mildly. One of the side effects of record unemployment in Britain at that time was that people took any work they could find to avoid the dole queue, rather as I had been forced to under orders from my mother. Unfortunately, it meant that some people who weren't well suited to nursing not only joined the profession, but stayed for years and progressed up the ranks. Psychiatric nursing was marginally better paid than general nursing (as is still the case today, just about), which exacerbated the problem in mental health hospitals by attracting staff who were more interested in their pay packet than the patients. This sister was the worst example I ever came across. Judy had no time for our patients and I never saw her show any compassion. If Sister Kane could have seen her saying, 'Sorry, my shift's ended, I'll deal with this tomorrow,' instead of sitting down and reassuring a patient, she'd have given her a proper good tongue-lashing, and rightly so.

To add insult to injury, Judy was also well known for arriving at work on a Tuesday with empty shopping bags and leaving the hospital with them full to the brim at the end of her shift. We all knew what she was up to. Tuesday was 'stores day', when supplies of tea, biscuits, coffee, butter, milk, soap, disinfectant, scrubbing brushes and so on arrived on the ward. There were no such things as budgets and inventories back then, the shelves being regularly restocked with whatever was needed, no questions asked. Shamelessly, Judy helped herself to as much as she could carry. She was not alone in this. There were quite a few others who also left with bulging bags on a Tuesday, including some of the cleaners who had the audacity to run a Sunday market stall where they sold off their swag at cut prices. When this eventually came to light the cleaners were sacked, though there were no other repercussions and we'd never know how much they had cost the NHS over the years. I found the whole thing quite embarrassing as well as unethical. Suffice to say, I couldn't *wait* to discover what our unpleasant sister had to apologise to the vicar for; and when I found out, it certainly didn't disappoint.

We had a young woman on the ward who had been picked up by the police for 'sexually disinhibited behaviour' in the street. From the moment she arrived, Delores had been asking the male nurses if they fancied her, or wanted to have sex with her. 'You do, don't you?' she'd say. 'I know you do!'

Today was Sunday, the day when our handsome young vicar paid his regular weekly visit to the ward. As soon as Delores saw him being let through the entrance door she was on a mission, launching herself at speed down the length of the corridor and then sliding towards him on her knees, like a jubilant footballer celebrating a goal. When Delores came to a stop her legs were splayed at the vicar's feet, at which point she screamed, 'Fuck me, Vicar! Fuck me now!'

The mortified vicar flushed so red even his scalp was glowing under his white-blond hair, but what made me laugh the most was Sister Judy's desperate embarrassment that this had happened on her watch.

Sam's parents visited him that afternoon, arriving at the door with a carrier bag filled with glossy car and motorbike magazines, his favourite Fry's Chocolate Cream bars and a brand-new pair of Reebok trainers.

'We can't thank you enough for all the wonderful work you do here,' his mother said. 'We know he's in excellent hands.'

'I second that,' said his father, a very dapper chap in a well-cut suit. 'We're extremely grateful.'

Though plenty of people thanked us when they left, it was unusual to get thanks from parents whose child had only just been admitted.

'Thank you,' I smiled.

I was so proud of being a student nurse – I was a year into my training at this time – and the appreciation gave me a warm glow. However, I also felt a wave of sadness wash over me as I looked at Sam's parents. Despite being pristinely dressed in their Sunday best, they were a vision of abject pain and suffering, their torment dripping from every pore. Their consideration for me and the other members of staff made their situation all the harder to bear.

I found out more about Sam over a snatched coffee break with another colleague later that morning. He had been in and out of mental health units for several years, and on his last ward (an acute admission unit) he had perfected the art of convincing patients who were allowed out on unescorted visits to buy him packets of paracetamol, which he then proceeded to swallow in large quantities. Sam managed to do this on multiple occasions, though he always told the staff what he'd done immediately afterwards, so his life was never really in danger.

Paracetamol overdose is extremely dangerous, and even relatively small overdoses can cause liver damage and lead to death. Nowadays patients are treated with a drug called acetylcysteine which is given intravenously and virtually eliminates any liver damage. Unfortunately, the preferred antidote was much less sophisticated in the 1980s, and after being rushed to A & E on a blue light Sam would be made to swallow the drug Ipecac, which caused extreme vomiting. It was decided that moving him onto a locked ward was the only way to stop him accessing paracetamol and repeating this cycle. Of course, the majority of our patients were not allowed out on unescorted leave, although it did happen sometimes when they were making good progress or perhaps preparing to return to living in the community. We didn't routinely search these patients when they came back, but after Sam's arrival this had to change, and we were under strict instructions to search every patient returning to the ward.

I asked my colleague what she knew about Sam's family background, interested to know more about his parents. 'Dad's a company director, mum's a head teacher. Older brother, younger sister. No other mental health concerns in the family . . . damn!'

My colleague looked at her watch and promptly stubbed out her fag. 'Got to dash,' she said. 'Time to give Delores her meds. And we can't miss that, can we?'

'Definitely not!' I laughed.

I gradually started to build up quite a good relationship with Sam, playing lots of card games with him and telling him every car story I could think of. Most involved me breaking down in my old orange Mini in the most inconvenient places conceivable, the most embarrassing example being outside the fire station in town, which resulted in me being pushed out of the way by several very unimpressed firefighters.

I found Sam to be easy-going, bright and intelligent, and to all intents and purposes he was the model patient. He happily attended activity sessions like art, cookery and keep-fit classes organised by the occupational health therapist, and he always took his medication without complaint. Sam's parents visited daily, sometimes bringing in his older brother and little sister, all of whom clearly loved Sam very much.

A few weeks after he arrived the whole family turned up one Sunday with a bag full of board games, brought from home. Visits would generally take place in the lounge or dining room, where we could maintain observations at a distance, and this was the case with Sam. The family didn't object – on the contrary, they were grateful for everything – and they all took their places around a table in the dining room, smiling as Sam's little sister insisted they start by playing her favourite game, Operation. I thought what a lovely close-knit group they looked as I sat nearby and had a coffee. Sam wasn't doing very well in the game, I noticed, struggling to remove the funny bone and bread basket and all the other fiddly little 'ailments' without setting off the buzzer. Still, he took the thrashing by his siblings in good spirit.

'You're a natural,' he told his little sister. 'I reckon you could beat all the doctors in this hospital.'

'No,' she said. 'Daddy said all the doctors and nurses are very, very clever. I think what they will do is this.' Waving the tweezers over the cartoon patient's head, the little girl pretended to tweak something in his brain. 'The clever doctors will do a special operation on you, like this, and it will make you all better!'

If only it were that simple, I thought.

One morning I arrived on the ward to learn that the night staff had discovered Sam had been burning himself with his cigarettes. He had hundreds of tiny burns all over his chest, something that must have been going on for weeks but which only came to light because he was in pain, the burns having become infected. After that, Sam was no longer allowed to keep hold of his cigarettes and could only smoke under supervision, although even when he was being watched he continued trying to burn himself.

'Stop it, Sam,' I said, the first time I witnessed this. I was one of the nurses on duty in the TV lounge, keeping an eye on several patients, but Sam didn't seem to care who saw what he was trying to do.

He made a half-hearted attempt at trying to fight off the male nurse who intervened and took the cigarette from his hand, and then when he was eventually allowed another one he did the same thing again.

'Why are you doing this to yourself?' I asked.

Sam shrugged his shoulders and said nothing.

It was clear the only way we could prevent Sam from burning himself was to stop him smoking altogether, which he really struggled with. As well as being addicted to nicotine, Sam had a history of alcoholism, I learned. 'Sam acknowledges this is not a healthy way to manage his feelings,' it said in his notes, 'but at times he doesn't care.'

At the start of my next shift I discovered Sam had been found tying a chain of plastic carrier bags around his neck, although once again this was not a serious suicide bid. Sam was standing behind a curtain in the dining room and there were several members of staff around. He was also seen checking to make sure he would be noticed before he put the bags round his neck. Again, when a couple of nurses tried to stop him, he fought them off, or at least made a show of trying to do so. I never felt he really wanted to kill himself.

After this we were very careful to check Sam's room for plastic bags and we asked his parents not to leave any carrier bags behind after their visits. The next time they arrived with magazines and treats for Sam they carried them in their arms, a sight that brought a lump to my throat.

Sam's history of self-harm stretched back over many years, and

I'd learned that the reason he was moved to the acute admission ward where he took the paracetamol overdose was because his self-harm had become more extreme. After years of making small cuts on his arms and legs, Sam had slashed himself with a razor blade, opening up his thigh. 'Self-mutilation' was the phrase used in the notes that accompanied him to the acute admission ward.

Though we were observing Sam closely and making every effort to take away anything he might use to cut or harm himself in any way, in common with all persistent self-harmers Sam was adept at finding new ways to inflict pain and damage on his body. In the absence of carrier bags he attempted to strangle himself with items of clothing, and he prised the staples out of the magazines his parents brought him and gouged at his skin. When the magazines were removed, Sam dug his fingernails into old wounds, opening them up until they bled profusely, in the way Michelle had before she was put in the plaster cast.

Gary was on the ward at the same time as Sam, and it wasn't very long after he'd cut himself from his wrist to his shoulder in response to Marie taunting him about his 'pathetic' self-harm.

'That it, mate?' Gary said to Sam one day, puffing out his chest. 'They're just scratches, they are.'

Gary wasn't being malicious. He had simply seen a chance to be top dog for once, and he didn't have the foresight to think that history could repeat itself. Unfortunately, after that exchange Sam's self-harm intensified. He ripped open every old wound he could gouge his fingers into, including the worst of the burn scabs on his chest, and then he removed the blade from a safety razor he begged from another patient and mutilated his other leg with it.

I'll never forget accompanying Sam to A & E to have the gaping wound stitched up. It was twelve inches long and ran from the outside of his knee to his ankle – a very unusual place for anyone to cut themselves.

'I've got better things to be doing with my time,' the grumpy male doctor told him dismissively. 'I suppose you want pain relief now, do you?'

Sam, as white as a sheet, his clothes splattered with blood and with one foot swimming in a pool of congealing blood inside his new Reebok trainers, politely shook his head.

'No, no, I don't. I don't need anything.'

Sam was clearly in desperate need of pain relief and was trying to be brave and macho in the circumstances he found himself in, but before I could change his mind a nurse was already whisking him into a side room, where she began sewing Sam up without any anaesthetic, just as Gary had been treated. Sam was in absolute agony, tears rolling down his face, but he still didn't utter a word of complaint. It was one of the most barbaric things I ever witnessed, and if I had my time again I would never let this happen.

Christmas was just around the corner and the ward was teeming with visitors. Sam's whole family arrived one Saturday, bringing chocolates for all the staff and a wonderful card that expressed their heartfelt thanks. Sam had been with us for about two months, and at last things were going in the right direction. His care team had agreed that the best way to treat him was by administering sedatives, typically benzodiazepines like diazepam, and to put him under increasingly high levels of observation. Sam was still finding ways to self-harm, but the combination of his medication, keeping him away from cigarettes and the increased observations meant he was no longer carrying out the extreme self-harm and parasuicidal behaviour we'd seen.

Stuart, our James Bond wannabe, also had a visitor that day. We'd got to know his mother, Gladys, quite well, not least because she was nearly always well lubricated when she arrived on the ward, happy to tell us all her business whether we wanted to hear it or not. She'd had a flood in her flat that winter, and we'd heard chapter and verse about the difficulties she had had removing the sodden carpet. 'I thought, "Screw this,"' Gladys said. '"I'm an old lady. I'm not moving all that furniture."' When we asked what happened next, she proudly explained how she'd cut around her settee and Welsh dresser with a Stanley knife, and only thrown away the carpet she could manage to lift.

While Sam's parents sat quietly in a corner of the dining room, Stuart's mother plonked herself centre stage in the lounge at the other end of the corridor. In addition to Stuart, also assembled were Seth, Nikolajs, Agatha, Marie, Gary, Rex and Benedict. A Christmas film was on the TV and everyone was quiet and contented after teatime, Nikolajs and Rex nodding off beside each other on one of the settees and Agatha wedged in next to Benedict on another, seemingly oblivious to the fact it was high time I told him, 'You smell!' We didn't know it at the time, but a scene like this would soon slide into history, individual chairs gradually replacing sofas so that patients in mental health units didn't come into physical contact with one another.

All the staff on duty were running around like blue-arsed flies that day, but they still found the time to share a drink with nurses who popped in from the other wards, and to go and have a drink with colleagues in other parts of the hospital. Ever since my first Christmas on Sister Kane's ward, I'd always enjoyed being in the hospital over the festive period. The long-term patients felt like family all year round, though the starkness and smells of the ward had a habit of reminding you where you were, most of the time. It was different at Christmas. The ward was decorated with tinsel and a tree, and tins of Quality Street and boxes of mince pies were devoured daily. Alcohol was in plentiful supply – if you worked over Christmas in the 1980s you would be drinking for most of the shift. It felt almost like Christmas at home, which was just as well, given that I spent five or even six days a week locked inside the ward, and often worked on Christmas Day.

Though Sam's admission had forced us to search the patients who returned from unescorted trips outside the hospital, none of the visitors to the unit were ever searched. This is in sharp contrast to today, when everyone is routinely searched and every visitor has their bag placed in a locker before they are allowed in. Drugs are a huge problem nowadays, something that was almost unheard of in the 1980s, although visitors to Ward 14 did sometimes manage to sneak in alcohol for their friends and family. On this occasion, Gladys had taken full advantage of the season and smuggled in dozens of bottles of Holsten Pils. By the time this was discovered, most of the patients in the lounge were either blind drunk or fast asleep, and afterwards Judy the sister had quite a bit of explaining to do.

As well as finding that the vast majority of patients had a history of abuse, it was not uncommon to discover family patterns repeating. In Stuart's case, his mother Gladys had a history of alcoholism and a diagnosis of schizophrenia. The contrast between Sam's mother and Stuart's mother could not have been starker or more apparent than it was that day. At the end of their visit, a couple of the nurses managed to steer Sam's family to the door without them noticing the impromptu booze-up on the ward. Once again, Sam's mum was the epitome of the kind and considerate mother, thanking the nurses and reassuring her son that she would be back tomorrow, perhaps for a game of Monopoly? Gladys, meanwhile, was escorted off the premises by two male nurses, having been given several strong cups of coffee and a stern warning never to bring booze onto the ward again. As they poured her into a taxi, Gladys shouted profanities at the nurses.

I'd learned something very interesting about Sam's past in the last few weeks, and seeing his mum's kind and brave smile that day made me think about his history. Sam's mum was not, in fact, his biological mother. Sam had been adopted at birth, just as his older brother had – each from different families – while their little sister

163

was the only biological child of their parents. Sam's birth mother was an alcoholic, I discovered, and his birth father was a prolific and extreme self-harmer with a history of depression and unusual parasuicidal behaviour. This information was recorded somewhere in Sam's ever-expanding file, but as far as I knew he was never made aware of it, his adoptive parents choosing to focus on the future, prepared to do anything in their power to help their son get better. Ever since he arrived they had been fighting hard for Sam to be moved to a more appropriate, long-term community-based unit, which thanks to their persistence happened very soon after this weekend. Ward 14 had served its primary purpose, stopping his access to paracetamol, and this was definitely the right move for Sam.

Marie, in sharp contrast to Sam, was all alone in the world. I will never forget how scared she looked when she arrived on the ward on her first day. Dressed in a huge, baggy tracksuit, the sleeves pulled halfway down her hands, this elfin-faced young girl looked like she wanted her clothes to swallow her up.

'Come with me, Marie,' I said. 'I'll take you to your room.'

Benedict and Rex had just left the dining room and they stopped in their tracks on either side of the corridor, silent and unsmiling as they eyed the new arrival. The two men were each at least three times as wide as this very slight teenager, and Rex's face was contorted into an involuntary, lecherous grimace. As we filed between the two men, I saw Marie draw in her slim shoulders, the way you might when it's dark and cold and you have to walk through a narrow passageway, afraid of what's lurking on the walls.

I felt desperately sorry for Marie. She was just fifteen years old and had come to us via a court diversion scheme after failing to provide an address she could be bailed to, and showing signs of mental distress. This was exactly what had happened to Billy, the young lad Seth terrorised, though in Marie's case she'd stolen a Marathon bar from WHSmith rather than a packet of Walkers crisps from Superdrug. At least once the doctors had prepared a report on her mental health condition she'd be sent to a more suitable facility, I thought, and hopefully as swiftly as Billy had been.

It's a frightening experience for a child who is already in a distressed state to find themselves on an adult mental health ward of any kind, though it was decades in the future – 2006 – before Tony Blair's government would pledge that no child under sixteen would be treated on an adult psychiatric ward 'within two years'. Your maths doesn't need to be any better than Ralph's to work out that that promise should have been honoured by 2008. Despite this, the practice continues to this day, a recent Care Quality Commission report showing that in 2020/21, 249 under-eighteens were admitted to adult psychiatric wards – a rise of 30 per cent on the year before.

Looking at Marie, I thought back to how distressing it was for me as a seventeen-year-old employee, finding myself on an open psychiatric ward for the first time. How must it feel for her, a vulnerable child on a locked ward, one full of potentially dangerous patients? I noticed her looking sideways at the dishevelled and disturbed trickle of men we passed along the corridor, her face etched with anxiety.

'Where do those men sleep?' she asked when I showed her to her bedroom.

'Down the corridor on the opposite side of the unit. Don't worry,' I said, trying my best to reassure her, 'this ward is very well staffed and there are lots of nurses here to look after you.'

Marie's history was heartbreaking, and what had happened in her past made her admission to Ward 14 all the more inappropriate. She came from a deeply troubled background, one that involved extreme sexual abuse by her mother's many partners – a mother who was herself abused, very vulnerable and couldn't give her daughter the protection she needed. Marie was eventually excluded from school after multiple violent outbursts, and to escape the continued sexual abuse and neglect at home, she ran away to London when she was just fourteen years old.

To compound Marie's situation, at the time of her admission the majority of the patients on Ward 14 were male, as were most of the nurses. I continued trying to offer reassurances, explaining how the patients were observed at night, but nothing I said could alter the fact she had to sleep locked up under the same roof as this unknown group of male patients.

'When you've unpacked, would you like to come and watch TV with me in the lounge?' I asked after showing her into her bedroom. '*Blockbusters* is on soon. I love that show.'

Marie shook her head and pulled her sleeves over the ends of her fingertips.

'You know the one,' I went on. '"Can I have a 'P', please, Bob?"'

My attempt at raising even the glimmer of a smile fell flat.

'I'm OK, thanks,' she said. 'I'll just stay in my room if that's all right, put my stuff away.'

I saw her looking around the sparse room, her eyes settling on the bolts fixing the wardrobe to the floor. 'Can I use this?' she asked, opening the wardrobe doors.

'Yes, of course.'

I helped her unpack her small holdall of belongings. This was something I was obliged to do because we had to check that patients didn't bring any banned items onto the unit, such as nail files, scissors, lighters and pens. Marie's few pairs of jogging pants, sweatshirts and washed-out collection of underwear barely filled even a quarter of the wardrobe, and I couldn't help thinking of my own overstuffed wardrobe, and how, as a teenager like Marie, I used to steal clothes from one of my sisters. The door to my sister's wardrobe was always locked to stop me doing just this, but little did my sister know that I had learned to stretch out a wire coat-hanger, poke it up through the bottom of the wardrobe and hook off her best Chelsea Girl and Topshop garments. The memory of my many heists, and how I would sneak out of the house in the outfits I 'borrowed' from my sister, usually made me laugh, but not today. When I left Marie in her room I felt a similar pang to the one I felt when I left Agatha behind and went out dancing.

For the rest of the day, whenever I had a moment to myself, I found my mind returning to the uncomfortable and very upsetting gulf between our teenage experiences. At Marie's age I was having dates with boys, sneaking into pubs and getting someone to buy me half a lager. I grew up with my two sisters, who I adored and argued with in equal measure. We went on holiday to Butlin's every year, and there were images in my head of donkey rides on the beach, fancy-dress competitions and teatimes in the big, noisy canteen that never failed to warm my heart. I remembered the messages that would be given out regularly over the tannoy, a redcoat announcing, 'Baby crying in chalet ten'. This was for the benefit of parents who had left their kids asleep and gone to the bar or the cabaret, though my mum and dad had so little money that after they put me and my sisters to bed, all they could afford to do was go and watch TV in the television hall. Mum didn't tell me that until many years later; nothing was going to burst our childhood bubble of innocence and joy.

Unfortunately, diagnosing Marie's mental health condition proved difficult for the doctors. In the weeks to come they variously described her as having borderline personality disorder (BPD), depression, anxiety and obsessive-compulsive disorder. She was prescribed diazepam to improve her low mood and alongside this a comprehensive care package was put in place, including weekly sessions with our female psychologist (a new appointment, and not a popular one as all the nurses, myself included, thought she was fairly incompetent) and a weekly audience with our very superior male consultant psychiatrist (unfortunately, as well as the vast majority being male, most of the psychiatrists I worked with were cut from a similarly grand cloth to this one).

Marie also had a busy timetable of music, physical exercise and art therapy classes arranged by the very efficient, proactive and jolly occupational therapist, the same one who did a great job of engaging Sam in those activities.

BPD is an all-encompassing diagnosis, and in my experience one often given to women when the medical staff can't understand why someone is behaving in a particular way. Marie certainly displayed many of the characteristics that apply to BPD, such as unstable moods that might make her withdraw and behave in a reclusive way one minute and then have a burst of anger the next, often one that came from nowhere. 'Is it too much to fucking ask for some fucking porridge?' she would shout. 'Why have we only got cereal? I don't want fucking cornflakes!' Then she would throw her bowl down on the floor, or start screaming, 'Give me some fucking tablets!' Sometimes the ranting and screaming led to physical violence, Marie kicking and punching the laundry-room door, for instance, if she wanted to use the washing machine and it wasn't possible at that moment.

The first time Jonathan had met her, Marie had rushed at one of the other nurses and tried to stub a cigarette out on her face. Jonathan reacted quickly, forcibly restraining Marie, though it wasn't easy. She was a lot stronger than she looked and put up quite a fight, spitting insults at everyone as she kicked and screamed and told Jonathan to 'fucking get off me!' It was a bad start, and one that made Marie hate Jonathan with a passion.

Marie had struggled to form relationships throughout her

life – another BPD marker – and in common with Gary she didn't have a friend in the world, or a single relative who would visit or phone. Marie also suffered acute feelings of loneliness and isolation – yet another feature of BPD, though as I said to Jonathan, what child wouldn't be moody, angry and feel lonely and abandoned if they'd endured a life like Marie's, and then had the misfortune to find themselves locked in a psychiatric hospital with all these strange and frightening men?

I wasn't alone in voicing my opinion that Marie shouldn't stay on Ward 14 a minute longer than necessary. A community-based setting would be far more appropriate, one where she could live as normal a life as possible, with a strong network of support. Unfortunately, while the doctors continued to struggle to agree on a clear diagnosis there was nothing the nursing staff could do but leave them to their job and get on with ours. However, it wasn't just Jonathan who had a tough time connecting with her. For the first few weeks, we were all struggling to engage with Marie in any way at all, let alone form a therapeutic relationship. Any offers to play games or go for a walk around the grounds were rebuffed and Marie spent as much time on her own as she could, in her room or watching TV in the small lounge, the hood of her sweatshirt pulled up and her handless sleeves wrapped protectively around her body. She barely said a word to any other patients, although Agatha was an exception, just about.

'You don't like them?' Aggie asked, watching Marie push mushy peas round her plate at teatime.

'I do with fish and chips but not with chops and mash,' Marie answered.

After that the two young women always exchanged a few words when the opportunity arose, though I wondered if Marie only responded to Agatha because she felt intimidated by her and wanted to show her she respected her.

One day, a month or so after her admission, Marie walked into the small lounge with spots of blood dripping from under the left sleeve of her sweatshirt.

'What have you done?' I said, my face falling.

'Cut myself. It's only a small cut, on my arm.'

Seth shouted at me to get out of his way as I sprang out of my seat and rushed to Marie's side, blocking his view of a game of pool between two other patients.

'Get on!' Seth said, waving his stick at me.

'You get on,' I said silently to myself as I led Marie away to clean her up and dress her wound.

We were aware that Marie had a history of self-harm, and that she had been self-harming ever since she arrived, typically by digging her nails into old wounds and on one occasion using a pencil to gouge a long but thankfully shallow gash in her arm. As with all patients in this situation, all we could do was keep a close eye on her, encourage her to talk to us and keep sharp objects away from her. Clearly we'd failed this time, as she had managed to pull off the too-familiar trick of convincing (or begging) a newly arrived patient to 'loan' her his safety razor.

171

About a month or so after she cut her arm, I was watching TV with Marie when *Grange Hill* came on.

'I hated school,' I piped up.

Marie looked astonished.

'Did you?'

'Absolutely. My mum used to drop me off at the front gate and I'd walk through the school and go straight out the back door. Then I'd go off and have a cig, or spend my pocket money in the corner shop.'

Marie laughed her head off. 'I didn't expect that,' she said.

This proved to be an unexpected breakthrough after weeks on end of chattering about whatever teenage stuff I could think of that might spark Marie's interest, like what music she was into or her favourite shows on TV. She had told me she loved Joan Collins in *Dynasty* so I tried to watch the show with her whenever I could, and on several occasions I offered to do her hair and make-up, as I did with Agatha. Up until now Marie had always refused and held me at arm's length, but after this conversation about school she asked if I could not just style her hair, but dye it for her.

'Of course,' I said. 'What colour are you thinking?'

'Purple,' she said, without hesitation.

Now it was my turn to say, 'I didn't expect that,' adding that I thought it was a very good choice indeed. From then on, dyeing Marie's hair became a regular ritual. Again, this would not be allowed today – you can't even apply suncream to a patient when the sun is cracking the flags – but of course times were different, and from that day on I dyed Marie's naturally fair hair pink, red, blue, green and every shade in between. I also spent hours painting her nails and trying to copy, amongst others, Boy George's make-up, with mixed results.

The next time Marie self-harmed, another few months on, she cut her face, scratching tiny criss-crosses on her cheeks and forehead with an opened-out staple. I'd never seen a patient cut their face before and I was shocked and upset to see her in such a state.

'Why did you do that, Marie?' I asked as I gently cleaned away the spots of blood with antiseptic wipes.

It was a question I'd asked after she cut herself in other places, but Marie had never answered me before now, always responding with a shrug or by saying, 'I dunno.'

'I suppose I cut myself for lots of reasons,' she said thoughtfully, staring past me and looking at nothing in particular. 'Sometimes I like to see the blood. I think that's what I did today. Sometimes I just enjoy pulling my cuts open. I do that when I'm bored, if I'm honest. It's a habit, Belinda.'

She looked me in the face now, and I asked her how she *felt* when she cut herself. It was a big question, but Marie didn't miss a beat.

'Better,' she said, studying my reaction with her pale-blue eyes. 'It's a release of emotions that's so *powerful*.' There was a pause as she exhaled, as if with the relief of letting this truth out. 'I feel happy, but then, I suppose I feel sad and disappointed in myself. That's what usually happens, in the end.'

I nodded. 'How do you feel right now?'

'Bad,' she said, her hands disappearing up her sleeves and her chin dropping to her chest. 'I wish I hadn't done this, really.'

By this time, Jonathan had also managed to form a good thera-peutic relationship with Marie, something that had taken a lot of patience and determination on his part. He was never one to shy away from telling Marie when she was in the wrong and so they argued quite a lot, but I think she had gradually come to realise that Jonathan cared about her, and that that was why they fell out.

I remember the day I knew his hard work had finally paid off. Back in the day Jonathan had bright blond hair and wore very tight jeans, and he always carried a plastic comb in his back pocket, which I and the other student nurses used to pull out to annoy him. He would always laugh even though we knew it really wound him up, and of course that made us do it all the more. I told Marie this story one day and she teased Jonathan about it the next time she saw him.

'How did he react?' I said.

'I could tell he was wound up,' she said. 'But he still laughed!'

'Good for him,' I said.

'Yeah,' Marie said. 'He's one of the good ones, isn't he?'

I'd never heard her pay any of the nurses a compliment, and this was praise indeed.

'You're not wrong there, Marie,' I smiled. 'And I'm so pleased to hear you say that.'

About six months into her stay, Marie had become adept at per-suading the junior doctors to change her medication on a regular basis, seemingly whenever the mood took her. This unnecessary disruption in routine was frustrating to the nursing staff, and a lot of my colleagues (and particularly those who had stopped putting in the effort when they got nothing back) were starting to lose all patience with her.

As the doctors continued to grapple with a definitive diagnosis for Marie, the male nurses in particular started to mutter that she was not 'mentally ill' at all, but rather a damaged female, and one who was 'playing the system' and 'being manipulative'. Gary had come in for similar criticisms, of course, but being a man and without a BPD label attached to him, I saw that he was less vilified and generally shown more sympathy than Marie.

It had also become obvious that Marie's unpopularity intensified whenever she openly self-harmed after a period of calm. 'She knows exactly what she's doing,' some nurses complained. 'She's a little madam, that one. She likes the attention.'

I think it's true that Marie did indulge in some deliberate self-sabotage whenever she was making good progress, probably because after so many months on the unit the prospect that she might have to move out and start again somewhere else had begun to frighten her. This was an upsetting realisation; despite Ward 14 being such an inappropriate place for a damaged child like her, she had already become institutionalised, to a degree. However, our job was to help Marie, not judge her unkindly. On my nurse training course I was being taught to focus on need, behaviour and symptoms rather than diagnosis. The example given in the classroom was that if someone was expressing a paranoid delusion, for instance, we should focus on the emotional content of that delusion above all else. When I applied this logic to Marie it meant focusing on what she was going through and feeling in the moment, what she needed from us in the here and now, and working out how we could help her feel better. The list of inconclusive diagnoses the doctors came up with, and her apparently orchestrated self-harm, should not interfere with how the nurses cared for her, though I'm afraid it did. Marie became quite a divisive character on the ward, with about half of my colleagues taking against her.

This all came to a head during a game of pool one evening, Marie suddenly started to tell Jonathan about her time living on the streets in London. Whenever a patient discloses significant information about their history we add it to their file, and I can remember the intense sadness I felt when Jonathan told me what he had written down, based on their long conversation.

'Marie's days were spent begging for money to feed and clothe herself, and when she had enough cash she would go to a public toilet, wash, put on her new clothes and throw away the old ones before getting something to eat. If the weather was fine she sat in a park, and if it rained she rode on the tube until it was time to find somewhere to sleep for the night. Like many homeless young people, Marie was robbed, hit, spat on, urinated on and sexually abused on the streets.'

I was saddened all over again to discover that this information didn't soften some of the hardest hearts amongst my colleagues, or make them reconsider their attitude towards her in any way.

Marie soon slipped into another phase, begging some of the nurses for more of the already hefty doses of benzodiazepines she was on – usually diazepam. We could all see that she did this when she was bored, or just wanted to completely zone out for the day. Though I didn't endorse her behaviour (and wouldn't have given her the extra drugs), I could at least understand it. There were clearly deep-seated psychological factors at play, and what teenager didn't pull a few stunts? However, some of the other nurses were scathing about this behaviour, using it as yet more evidence of Marie being a manipulative, untrustworthy patient who was abusing our service.

Diazepam creates a sense of calm by increasing 'calming chemicals' in your brain and creating a sedative effect, and it is also highly addictive. When Marie was genuinely feeling very low she craved diazepam, and as it was prescribed 'PRN' some nurses would give it to her to stop her nagging and keep her quiet. Others dished it out because they felt sorry for her and couldn't bring themselves to say no. Both were bad practice, and one day Marie had been given so much diazepam that she was incontinent and couldn't walk. The following day we had her prescription changed to a tapering-off dose before discontinuing it. This resulted in a few weeks of very angry behaviour from Marie, and she had several violent outbursts, all directed at members of staff. One day she was trying to force her way into the charge nurse's office and when I tried to stop her, talking to her and gently taking hold of her arm, she turned round and hit me in the face. I wasn't really hurt and I wasn't annoyed at Marie, but I was very angry with my colleagues who had contributed to her being in this state.

By the time Marie had been with us for a year – and had turned sixteen – she felt like another member of my extended family, which is hardly surprising given that I spent most of my week at work, locked on the ward with her, just as I did with Agatha. Along with many of my colleagues, I'd never stopped lobbying for Marie to be cared for in a community setting, where she could enjoy a more normal life and even get a job. But whatever diagnosis the doctors came up with next, as long as Marie continued to self-harm those in charge concluded that she was too great a risk to herself to be released from the ward. I could understand their fears.

Unfortunately, Marie's self-harm had intensified and was gradually becoming more brutal. She had started to cut her whole body with razor blades and anything else she could get her hands on, including the sharpened handle of a toothbrush. There was scarcely a patch of skin that had not been opened up, and not only was Marie prolific in her self-harm, but some of the cuts she made were so extreme she looked like she'd been mutilated with a butcher's knife.

Even if you put Marie under 24/7 observations, 365 days a year, the members of her care team agreed, you would still have had to sit on her or hold her hands down to stop her self-harming or opening up old wounds. Not only that, but continuous observations would have had a significant emotional impact on Marie, not least because male as well as female staff would be required to watch her every move. It was a hideous situation.

Marie told me that sometimes when her cuts started to heal she 'enjoyed' ripping them open all over again, pulling the skin apart with her nails and digging her fingers into the gaping wound. Her face glistened with dozens of small scars and she also had scabs on her hands where she occasionally burnt herself with cigarettes, or repeatedly rubbed her clothing onto her skin to cause friction burns. 'I do that when I just want to hurt myself, Belinda,' she said. 'It doesn't let my feelings out.' I'd heard Sam say a similar thing once, about burning being a predominantly physical act of self-harm, as opposed to the emotional release of bloodletting.

Marie tried to hide much of her self-harm, but sometimes she would deliberately walk into the lounge or appear on the corridor with blood on her face, or soaking through her top, as she had done early on. Then she'd just stand there staring vacantly into space, waiting to be cleaned up and bandaged all over again. On some occasions she was taken to the on-call doctor or to A & E to be stitched up and I went with her whenever I could, always issuing strict instructions that she must be given adequate pain relief, which thankfully she was.

As a team we had been trying for a long time to encourage Marie to manage her emotional needs in a less devastating way than by literally tearing her body to pieces. Teaching her to breathe in and out in a deep and calming way when she began to feel tense was one of the strategies I had started to use with her. I also reinforced everything she learned on an anger management course about identifying triggers that made her angry and using various techniques to reduce her emotional and physiological responses to those feelings. The success of this was variable. 'Sometimes I *want* to feel anger,' Marie told me. 'I don't want to control it, Belinda. I want to express it.'

I could empathise with the ethos of what she was saying. Sister Judy continued to make my blood boil. She was such an uncaring and self-centred person, and she also had a very irritating habit of closing her eyes dramatically whenever she complained about something. If someone had told me to take a deep breath and walk the other way when she angered me, I'd have told them no, I need to vent my frustration. And I did every time, because while Judy's eyes were closed I always took the opportunity to stick my tongue out at her and pull the most disparaging face I could while she wasn't looking.

I wouldn't have dreamed of sharing that story with Marie – it was so trivial compared to what she was going through – but I did empathise, telling her I heard what she was saying and that I did understand her need to express her anger sometimes. 'Thank you, Belinda,' she said. 'At least someone listens. Sometimes I might as well talk to the wall.'

By the time Marie was seventeen the professionals in her care team decided it would be a good idea to let her do some 'normal' activities, like going to the cinema and for meals out.

Hallelujah!

I was one of the nurses who accompanied Marie into town on several occasions and she always seemed to enjoy herself, particularly when her favourite Chinese food was on the menu. That said, after nearly two years on the ward Marie was so unused to going out that I think she found it quite a challenge too, often becoming very moody when it was time to get ready and making pessimistic comments about how the film might be rubbish, or the food disappointing. 'Is it worth it?' she'd say. This was perfectly understandable, as we'd all discover many years in the future when the COVID pandemic took away our liberty and, in some cases, our confidence to venture back into the community as we had before. I also saw that, however much she'd enjoyed the trips out, Marie always looked relieved when we returned to the safety of the ward. And that is what Ward 14 had become. It was a safe haven, a place that gave her asylum from a world that had failed her so catastrophically. A place Marie saw as home, or the closest thing she had to a home.

When her eighteenth birthday was looming, Jonathan and I asked permission to take Marie out to a nightclub. This was something we were both keen to do and had talked about for a while, amongst ourselves and with Marie. She was totally on board with it. Marie had missed out on so much and had never once celebrated her birthday growing up, and Jonathan and I successfully argued that this was a chance for her to have fun and feel like all the other teenagers for a change. The care team agreed, trusting in Jonathan and me and the strong relationship we'd built up with

Marie over what now amounted to two and a half years. I don't remember being given any specific instructions or orders. The night was ours, and all we had to do was take good care of Marie and bring her safely back to the ward at the end of the evening.

'What colour are we doing your hair for the big night out?'

'Shocking pink, please!' Marie replied.

'I love it! And I have the perfect nail varnish to go with that. You're going to look fantastic!'

We were going to a small club in town where a DJ was throwing a 'Club Tropicana' disco night. We'd been planning what we would wear for weeks, and in the end Marie and I settled on Bananarama-style outfits with bandanas in our hair, and Jonathan wore a white T-shirt and black leather jacket with his tight jeans (complete with the obligatory plastic comb in the back pocket). We all thought we looked the bee's knees and were buzzing on the bus into town, but as soon as we sat down at a table in the club, Marie went very quiet and looked uncomfortable. 'Don't tell anyone it's my birthday, will you?' she said, looking at all the teenagers shimmering through the dry ice on the dance floor.

'Of course not, if you don't want us to.'

The music was great and the atmosphere wasn't half bad, though it wasn't quite as lively as Benny's on a Monday and we were only sipping Cokes and shandies, careful not to let Marie get drunk.

'Shall we go now?' she said, dragging nervously on a cigarette.

We'd only been there for an hour and a half and the night had barely got going, but I think the whole event, including the build-up, had been a bit too much for Marie. Afterwards I realised the night out might have made her feel even more isolated from her peers, though that's only a guess, as she didn't ever want to talk about it again.

On numerous occasions, Marie had admitted to me and others that she liked being cared for after she self-harmed, and our psychologist (as unpopular and ineffective as ever) decided this was a 'maladaptive thought process', and that Marie needed to find a different way to feel cared for, one that didn't involve her abusing herself. As a result a bold new strategy was put in place, one the psychologist believed would finally help Marie manage her self-harming behaviour.

I heard about this over the six o'clock tray and instantly lost my appetite for buttered toast. Marie could ask the nurses for a surgical pack if need be, or for help with suturing a wound, but we were not to respond to her self-harm unless she specifically asked us for help. Even then we should communicate with her as little as possible and encourage her to clean her wounds up herself, using antiseptic wipes provided in her room.

'Give me strength,' one of my colleagues said. 'What claptrap is this?'

I couldn't agree more. This was an experimental approach, and in my opinion lacked any level of care and compassion.

'That's kind of the point, Belinda,' one of my colleagues said, a comment that made me go cold.

The new strategy didn't start well. Marie didn't clean her wounds properly and they became infected, and a couple of weeks down the line she didn't tell us when a slash on her abdomen needed medical attention. When this large, jagged wound became infected Marie ended up on IV antibiotics, but still we were told to press on with the plan. The psychologist's rationale was that when Marie mutilated her abdomen she had experienced an 'extinction burst' – a fairly common phenomenon whereby a patient's unwanted behaviour increases in intensity before it reaches a peak and then goes away.

'In other words,' Jonathan said, as pissed off with the psychologist as I was, 'we've all got to sit around watching it get worse before it gets better. Great!'

I found it unbearable, and I had no faith whatsoever in the extinction burst theory. Not only was it unscientific, in my opinion it was cruel, and treating a patient this way went against everything I and every other nurse had been taught: 'The very first requirement in a hospital,' wrote Florence Nightingale, 'is that it should do the sick no harm.'

I was sitting in the lounge one evening with a couple of patients and two nurses, shouting out answers to *Blockbusters*, when Marie crept slowly and quietly in and sat down beside me. I turned towards her to say hello. What I saw caused my heart to miss a beat. I took hold of her hand.

'Phone the on-call doctor and dial 999,' I said to one of my colleagues, who recoiled in shock when she turned to face us.

Marie's grey T-shirt was completely soaked in blood and a

necklace of congealed red jelly ran from ear to ear across her slender neck.

'It's going to be all right,' I said, my arm around Marie's back as I told her we would get her all the care and attention she needed.

Marie was pale and silent, but she was breathing evenly and this had clearly happened some time earlier. 'It's going to be all right,' I repeated. 'Help is on its way.'

She gave me a faint smile. 'We're all here for you,' I went on. 'Don't worry, help is coming. We will get you sorted out, Marie. We will take care of you.'

The two other nurses accompanied her to the hospital and later on, when all my other jobs were done, I stood silently in the charge nurse's office with Neil. He knew exactly what I was thinking even before I said it.

'I can't do this, Neil. I'm not doing it any more.'

Neil nodded slowly and silently handed me the last three cigarettes in his packet.

Before I left for the evening I heard a couple of newly admitted patients gossiping about Marie's 'suicide attempt' and the fact she had 'slashed her throat'.

'This was not a suicide attempt,' I wanted to shout, but instead I reassured them that she was being well cared for and that they did not need to worry, or talk about Marie any more.

She had twenty-eight stitches in her wound. It was certainly true that Marie had slashed across her throat, but this was very much an act of parasuicide. Marie desperately needed help, yet this

185

vulnerable young woman had to go to these appalling lengths to show us how much trouble she was in, and how much she needed us to pay attention.

We had failed Marie, and when she came back to the ward with a grotesque, untidy scar across her throat I could have wept. She was in a far worse state than she had been in when she arrived almost three years previously, not one part of her body unscarred and much of her skin puckered and mesh-like after being torn and cut open on so many occasions.

Before long Marie was moved to another secure ward and then another, meeting new teams of people who would fail her all over again. As is often the case, even with patients you have nursed over a long period of time, I was not working on the day Marie finally left and I didn't get to have a last moment with her. Jonathan did, and my heart was in my mouth when he told me what happened. Marie had got up earlier than usual, before the night shift finished, and she asked Jonathan if she could have a word with him in private.

'Do you remember when I tried to stub out my cigarette in that nurse's face and you restrained me?' she said.

'I do, very well.'

'Well, you hurt me so much when you grabbed me that when you left the room I cried.'

'I'm sorry,' Jonathan started.

'No,' Marie said. 'I'm not asking you to say sorry, I haven't finished. I hated you when I arrived, and I hated you for a long time. But over these years I have realised that everything you have done for me since I got here is because you care for me, and you have always done what you think is best for me even if it caused us to fall out.'

'Thank you,' Jonathan said, taken aback. 'Thanks for saying this.'

'It's true, and I will miss you. Thank you for everything.'

Jonathan put his arms around her and hugged her tightly.

All these decades on, this final image of Marie never fails to make me feel emotional. Just like the barrel of plaster cast placed so crudely around Michelle's middle, the treatment Marie was given was of its time, and inappropriate even then. Marie should never have been placed on our ward or stayed as long as she did and I'm still overwhelmed with sadness whenever I think about what happened to her. Nowadays this would not happen to a patient like her and I take some comfort from that, reminding myself to be grateful for the progress we have made in caring for patients who self-harm.

CHAPTER 6

'The patients have a great time!'

I could hear Val Doonican's dulcet tones before I reached Lena's door. He was crooning his way through 'If I Knew Then What I Know Now', as he did every morning from the vinyl LP on her old wooden-based record player. I could already picture the scene in her tiny bedroom, because it was exactly the same every day, without fail. The first thing Lena did when she got up in the morning was create a makeshift shrine to her singing idol, arranging her precious collection of ornaments, photos and memorabilia around the record player. On the walls were her favourite photos of the twinkly-eyed Irishman, taken from newspapers and magazines that had run articles about his popular variety show. Val was often pictured in the press with his famous guests but Lena wasn't interested in anyone but him. She folded the newspapers strategically to hide Ray Charles, Lulu or Dudley Moore, making sure Val alone took centre stage as he smiled down from

189

the yellowing walls of her room. 'The only star,' Lena said often. 'Val Doo-ni-CAN, he is the only star!' Her Polish accent was thick and her English very limited, but Lena had perfected those two sentences.

When I knocked and went into her bedroom that morning Lena was doing what she always did after she'd built the shrine and was floating around and blowing kisses at each photo and ornament. She paused only to stroke Val's hair and tell him he was 'piękny człowiek' – a beautiful man.

I was seventeen when I first met Lena and she was a patient on Ward 5, one of the hospital's long-stay women's wards. Nobody was sure how long she'd been there, though I was told she was another of the patients who had arrived in England after the end of the Second World War, having no living relatives in Poland and not knowing a soul in the UK. She was sixty now, or thereabouts, and had been medicated with the old-fashioned anti-psychotic chlorpromazine for decades. She was probably in her early twenties when she was admitted, I was told. Certainly, Lena was already there when our longest-serving members of staff arrived, some of whom had been working at the hospital for thirty years or more.

There were forty-five women on Ward 5, all but Lena sleeping in one big dormitory. Most had become 'institutionalised', as Beryl, one of the kindly but slightly blunt older nurses, told me. I'd heard this word used many times, but now I'd started working with people who were clearly defined by it, I wanted to be sure I fully understood what it meant. 'Institutionalised behaviour is characterised by a person becoming less able to think and act independently,' I read in a nursing textbook. 'Hence they become totally reliant upon the institution and particularly the rules of the institution.'

There were dozens of grey-haired, prematurely frail and wrinkled patients on Ward 5. Lena didn't stand out to me in any way, and I was curious to know why she had the only single bedroom.

'It's what she's used to, love,' Beryl told me. 'And she's quite a difficult woman if she doesn't get her way.'

One of the other residents of Ward 5 was Josephine, a patient who had been admitted in the 1950s after giving birth 'out of wedlock', as it said in the faded notes in her file. Her family sent her newborn baby for adoption and had Josephine confined to the asylum, agreeing that she must be a 'moral imbecile' to have become pregnant when she was an unmarried teenager. I imagine that long before the trauma of her ordeal started to lessen – if it ever did – Josephine was already institutionalised, at least to some degree. Thirty-odd years on, she was irreversibly entrenched in hospital life, to the point where she couldn't function without it.

I'd always held the vague notion that institutionalised people would be zombie-like or look dead behind the eyes. It was true that some patients were disengaged to the point where they behaved in a robotic or emotionless way, but this was very largely due to their medication and not their institutionalisation.

Josephine was a loud and seemingly very cheerful character who was well known and well loved all around the hospital. I

191

say 'seemingly' because when I got to know her I had a feeling her cheery exterior was superficial, perhaps a coping mechanism Josephine had cultivated in order to deal with her incarceration. 'Time for your wash,' we'd say, and Josephine would be on her feet, making her way to the bathroom, apparently delighted to accept she had a rule to follow and the next segment of her day was mapped out for her.

Lena was quiet and reclusive by comparison, keeping herself (and Val) to herself and spending as much time as she could alone in her room, talking to her hero and constantly blowing him kisses. She only emerged to watch *The Val Doonican Music Show* on the BBC on a Saturday night, and at mealtimes, when she would take her regular place in the dining room. Tables of four were arranged in lines, and everyone sat in the same seat for years and years, nobody ever questioning this.

I couldn't imagine Lena being the 'difficult' patient Beryl described her as. Lena was a very small, slightly stooped woman, and she clearly had a lot of love in her heart. She always gave me a radiant smile when I said hello in the morning, and she was very grateful whenever I gave her a new clipping of Val, pilfered from an old copy of the *Radio Times* or a newspaper a visitor had brought in. 'Ah, the only star!' she would say appreciatively, fixing her grey eyes on Val's as she blew him a kiss. 'Val Doo-ni-CAN, he is the only star!'

Lena had a very strict routine before she went to bed, dismantling the shrine she'd built in the morning by carefully packing away every souvenir mug, coaster and faded seven-inch record sleeve, ready to start the whole ritual again tomorrow. As well as having the privilege of a single room, Lena was also excused from using the communal bathrooms to wash in. She was an 'obsessive-compulsive person', Beryl told me, and if everything wasn't in a certain place, or Lena's routine was upset in any way, she became 'distressed'. I'm not sure if this matronly older nurse was protecting my teenage sensibilities, but there was more to Lena's story than Beryl chose to tell me.

It was one of the other young nursing assistants who eventually filled in a few of the missing pieces, asking me if I knew that Lena was a survivor of a Nazi concentration camp. 'No,' I said to my colleague, unwelcome images flashing in my mind, courtesy of a black-and-white film I'd seen in a history lesson at school the year before. 'I didn't know that.'

I was so inexperienced that despite having met Olek on my first-ever ward – and knowing Lena was Polish, and had fled her country after the war – it had never even occurred to me that this might be her background.

'You don't want to see her when the memories come back,' the nursing assistant went on, her eyes widening. 'She screams and shouts, yelling stuff in Polish. You can't make head nor tail of most of it, but sometimes she says the words "Hitler" and "Jews". It's absolutely horrible, what she must have gone through.'

I didn't know what to say. Like most young people of my generation, to me the war felt like it happened hundreds rather than tens of years ago, and was now conveniently consigned to the pages of history books. I couldn't bear to think about what Lena had suffered, but my colleague was eager to tell me more, whether I liked it or not.

'You know why she's allowed to get washed in her bedroom?' she asked. 'Go on, have a guess.'

'Er, it's her routine?' I volunteered uncomfortably.

'Mmm. That's what I thought. Truth is, if Lena goes anywhere near the bathrooms she gets hysterical. It's the showers she's scared of the most. They *terrify* her. She completely loses it and starts shouting and screaming and trying to run away.'

The images this evoked really upset me, and I could think of nothing else for the rest of the day.

About a month after I learned about Lena's past I was in the town centre, shopping on my day off, when I spotted a poster outside the town hall. 'Val Doonican LIVE!' it screamed. Beneath the shimmering gold lettering was a picture of the man himself, sitting in his famous rocking chair, sporting one of his trademark knitted sweaters and a charming smile.

Lena is not going to believe this!

I could already see the poster on her bedroom wall, but I decided I was going to go one better than that. As soon as I arrived at work the next day I asked the sister if she would allow me to take Lena to see the show. Her eyebrows did a little jig and she let out a pensive 'hmm' sound, which didn't bode well. 'I get on well with Lena,' I said. 'I think she likes me, and because it's Val Doonican

I can't imagine she'd be any trouble at all. She'll be on her best behaviour, I know she will.' By the time I'd finished I'd delivered a pitch Alan Sugar would be proud of, and after hearing me out the sister gave me a promising smile and asked me to leave it with her.

To my delight, just before the end of my shift she called me into her office and said she'd made a decision.

'You have permission, Belinda, and I will leave it to you to tell Lena all about it.'

'Thank you, Sister,' I gushed. 'I'm so pleased! And I know Lena will be too.'

I made sure I bought the tickets before I broke the good news to Lena, and the look on her face when I told her was priceless. 'For me, Belinda? I see Val Doonican? This man, he is a star. I am so, so happy. Thank you, Belinda. Thank you! This is the big day of my life!'

Lena seemed totally unfazed at the prospect of upsetting her routine, not asking any questions about how we would get there or what time the show was on. Later that day I asked Beryl and another of the long-standing nurses on the ward if they remembered the last time Lena went out, and how it went. The pair of them looked at each other and shrugged as they tried to cast their minds back. 'I reckon it was that time we went to the switch-on of the Christmas lights,' Beryl's friend said eventually.

'When were that?' Beryl asked.

'Must have been 1974, 'cos I'd not long come back off maternity leave.'

I tried not to show my shock; I would have still been at primary school then, and Lena would have been in her early fifties.

There was no set policy or timetable for day trips, which meant outings were very often dependent on staff coming up with ideas and volunteering to accompany the patients, just as I had. The only regular event in the calendar was a holiday to North Wales, something that had been laid on every year since the 1970s. The hospital booked out the same seaside hotel across the summer months, and every week twenty different patients would be taken on the hospital minibus to sit in deckchairs on the sand, play in the penny arcades, eat ice cream and generally have a break from hospital life.

'If you don't behave you won't be going to Prestatyn,' I would hear Sister Brown threaten on many occasions, and she was always true to her word, because only those patients who were trusted not to be disruptive were allowed to go on holiday. This meant that the patients of Ward 14 were never on the guest list, unfortunately. When I first heard about the annual excursions I was quite fascinated, wondering how someone like Josephine, for instance, would cope with being thrust into a Welsh holiday resort after decades spent inside the hospital.

'The patients have a great time!' one of the chirpy male nurses told me enthusiastically. 'The staff too, I always volunteer. It's the other holidaymakers who have a problem, if anything. It's very obvious where we've come from and you do get some funny looks, but there isn't time to worry about that. You just have to crack on and get on with it.'

When 'the big day of my life' came round for Lena, I was really looking forward to taking her into town for the evening performance. She was very excited too, spending ages getting ready and changing out of her hospital-issue 'bundles', which that day consisted of a large blue cotton top that hung off her petite, bent frame and baggy, grey trousers that were rolled up several times around her ankles. I often thought Lena would have benefitted enormously if I'd got my way and was allowed to organise the bundles into sizes, rather than just 'tops and bottoms', as I was memorably ordered to do as a new recruit. Still, I thought at least this evening Lena had the chance to wear her own clothes for a few hours.

She put on some lipstick and the only skirt and jumper she possessed, items I was saddened to see looked so dated I would not have been surprised if she bought them on her last trip to town in the 1970s. When I went to collect her from her room she had also packed a large Kwik Save carrier bag, which was bulging at the seams.

'What's in there?' I asked.

'For Val Doo-ni-CAN!' Lena smiled. 'All for him. Gifts, all for him!'

'I'm not sure you need to take all that,' I said. 'What's in there, exactly?'

'Gifts, for him. All for him!'

Lena opened up the bag and proudly showed me her haul of 'presents'. It included several bottles of milk and an assortment

197

of sandwiches, cakes and biscuits, all lifted from the kitchen and dining room over the course of the previous week and squirrelled away in her room.

'No, no, Lena,' I said. 'You can't take all this into the town hall. It's very kind of you, but Val Doonican won't be able to have this, it won't be possible to give him these things.'

Her face fell.

'But I meet him? You tell me?'

Lena was not mistaken about this. To make the trip extra special I'd phoned the town hall, got hold of a number for Val Doonican's manager and asked if he would be kind enough to say hello to Lena in the interval. 'It will make her day,' I said. 'And quite probably her life.'

'No problem, Miss Gibson,' came the reply. 'I'm sure Mr Doonican will be delighted. Leave it with me. Come to the side of the stage when the interval lights come up.'

I was tickled pink and couldn't help sharing this news with Lena in advance, but now I wished I'd kept it to myself until we got to the show, because nothing I said would convince Lena to leave the gifts behind. 'Gifts for him,' she repeated, tightening her grip on the handles of the plastic bag. 'We meet. Me take gifts for him.'

It was time for us to get on the hospital transport and I had no choice but to give in, telling myself that I could deal with this when we got to the show. Hopefully, I thought, Lena would be so captivated by her crush she'd forget all about this carrier bag of contraband. Failing that, I would just have to 'get on with it', as mental health nurses had to do sometimes.

Lena was certainly captivated when she saw Val Doonican walk on stage. He was resplendent in an Aran polo-neck sweater and grey slacks and Lena was in raptures from the moment she set eyes on him. 'You the star!' she shouted from our second-row seat, standing up and waving her arms to attract his attention. 'You the star!'

He opened the show with one of his biggest hits, 'Walk Tall', which was greeted with a huge round of applause from the packed audience and an unexpected wolf whistle from Lena. The atmosphere was fantastic and her eyes were shining under the canopy of lights glowing overhead.

'Isn't this great?' I said, swaying to the music and giving her a smile.

'Yes!' she said. 'Me go give gifts now!'

I took a sharp intake of breath.

'No, no, Lena,' I said, reminding her that she would get to meet Val in the interval, and telling myself once again that I'd deal with this when the time came.

'Me go give gifts now!'

'No, Lena,' I said. 'We have to wait until the interval, but it's all arranged, don't worry.'

'Me go give gifts now!'

Give me strength!

'Enjoy the show, Lena. We will meet Val in the interval, I promise.'

She wasn't listening to a word I was saying and talked repeatedly over 'Walk Tall', asking again and again if she could 'give the gifts now'. In the end I felt I had no choice but to tune her out and focus on the show; nothing I said was getting through and we were disturbing other people in the audience.

As Val reached the end of his first number I glanced to my right to look at Lena and did a double take. My stomach lurched. While I'd been enjoying the end of the song she had decided to take the lyrics quite literally and was on her feet, 'walking tall' from her seat! Not only that, she had the overflowing carrier bag in her hand and looked like she meant business as she pushed hurriedly past the startled people sitting beside her.

'Lena!' I hissed. 'It's not the interval yet, come back!' My plea only made matters worse. Lena glanced back over her shoulder at me, a look of fierce defiance on her face. Worse still, realising I was on to her, she now made a break for it, quickening her pace and escaping into the aisle. As I followed, apologising to the people I had to climb over, Lena bolted as fast as she could towards the stage, reaching into the carrier bag as she went. To my horror, as soon as she was close enough to the front of the theatre, she started to launch missiles onto the stage. The first was an out-of-date pint of milk, the glass bottle shattering as it smashed into a speaker and slopped into a glinting white puddle at the side of the stage. Then came a rapid-fire assault of mouldy sandwiches, half-eaten biscuits and bits of old cake and cheese, pieces of which landed on Val's shiny black brogues. The singing star stood statue-still, staring in disbelief as the diminutive pensioner somehow managed to haul herself up onto the stage and launch another bottle in his direction, this one creating a lake of glass and milk around his feet. I was in hot pursuit, just two paces behind and with my heart beating like a drum as I reached the stage.

'Lena!' I implored. 'Stop it, stop it now!'

It was no use. Lena was on a mission and nothing was going to come between her and Val. The empty carrier bag was now discarded amongst the spilt milk and Lena was perilously close to the still-catatonic Val. I watched from feet away as she threw her arms around him as if he were her long-lost lover and proceeded to kiss his jumper, smearing it with her red lipstick. 'You star man! You the only star!'

The poor performer was *horrified*, his jaw dropping open as he tried to push Lena away as politely but firmly as possible. Meanwhile I had managed to get myself on the other side of Lena and was trying to pull her away from Val. It was like a scene in a comedy sketch and people in the audience were roaring with laughter, not sure if this was part of his variety act or not. It took the arrival of two furious security guards to give them the answer. One grabbed Lena and the other took hold of me, dragging us off the stage like a couple of rabid dogs. 'I can explain,' I said, flushed scarlet with embarrassment. 'I'm a nurse!' They were having none of it. The theatre lights had been turned up and the entire audience could see our shame as we were frogmarched down the centre aisle, hearing Val apologise for the 'unfortunate interruption' to the show. When we reached the front of the town hall, the guards wasted no time in throwing Lena and me unceremoniously into the street. 'And don't come back!' they warned. 'Disgraceful!'

I'd never been so humiliated in my life.

'That was awful,' I said when I'd managed to catch my breath. 'What did you do that for? We can't see the show now.'

'Yes,' Lena replied dreamily.

It was only then that I looked at her face. Unbelievably, Lena's eyes were still shining as brightly as they were at the start of the show. She was clearly not just undaunted by what had happened, she was absolutely delighted with the turn of events.

'I see him!' she grinned. 'I kiss him! Thank you, Belinda! Val Doo-ni-CAN, he is the only star!'

My experience with Lena didn't put me off organising trips, or taking patients out of the ward and into the town centre, or around the large hospital grounds. Quite the contrary. I loved it, even when things went wrong, which they unfortunately (and perhaps inevitably) had a habit of doing.

It wasn't very long after the Lena escapade when a patient from a male open ward gave us the slip at the busy street market in the town centre. We'd taken Fred out to buy new shoes but he had insisted on touring the market too. 'Excuse me, Nurses,' a young police officer said. 'We believe we have one of your patients over at the fruit and veg stall.' When my male colleague and I turned round, sure enough, there was Fred, stark naked, having stripped off every shred of his clothing. To add to the spectacle, he was waving around the parsnips and cucumbers, and a lot else besides. 'Belinda!' he said, seemingly oblivious to the horrified look on my face. 'Come and have a look at this!' I didn't know where to put myself.

In the end, several police officers helped us restrain Fred, put his clothes back on and return him to the hospital. Afterwards he talked about his cheeky stunt with great pride, describing the admiring looks he got from all the women around the stall. 'Admiring?' my friend said. 'I don't know where he got that from. They were all as mortified as us!' This was true, not least because Fred was a very old man, his skin more wrinkled than the dates and figs being sold by the scoop, weighed out on the big metal scales.

In years to come, when I was working on Ward 14, if the weather was sunny we sometimes closed the ward completely and all the patients and staff would sit on the grass outside having sandwiches and ice cream for tea. I really enjoyed those moments. You could always tell how much the patients appreciated leaving the confines of the ward, and it was a very welcome change of routine, giving us all something to look forward to and talk about afterwards.

Once in a while a patient would try to run off but the surrounding countryside was so vast we always managed to pull them back, usually straight away and always long before they reached the trees with the coloured tags on. We also went for walks and some of the patients and staff played tennis and football on the pitches, activities we were free to do without seeking authority from our superiors. There was the wood-panelled ballroom too, of course, with its sprung floorboards and impressive chandeliers, but this was a place where only 'well-behaved' patients would be taken to enjoy a dance or see the occasional show organised by the hospital. Inevitably, patients from other wards were much more likely to be trusted to attend such events than the inhabitants of Ward 14, and so, besides Ernie, I only ever took a handful of patients there over the years. They usually had a pleasant time, though they were still dressed in their bundles, which never felt right to me, surrounded as they were by the albeit faded glamour of the old ballroom.

Two memorable patients organised their own 'outings', in a roundabout sort of way.

'Give me a match, Belinda,' Joseph said. 'I want to smoke my cigar.'

'No, Joseph, you'll throw it on the floor.'

'I won't,' he said. 'Please do as I ask and give me a match, Belinda!'

I was eighteen years old, working on another one of the male open wards. Joseph always spoke to me as if I were a servant girl, at his beck and call, though I soon got to know him well enough not to take offence. This middle-aged man had been admitted to the hospital on several occasions, and I learned that experiencing 'grandiose episodes' was a symptom of his bipolar disorder, typically occurring during one of his manic phases. In Joseph's case, his grandiose episodes made him believe he was an important, world-leading businessman. He certainly looked the part, always arriving at the hospital in a sharp navy suit, dark-blue loafers and a crisp white shirt. Or at least that's how it looked from a distance, because when you got up close you realised the suit was stained and covered in dandruff from his greasy, unwashed hair, the collar of his shirt was ringed with muck and his shoes were fraying at the seams.

'I promise you, Belinda, I will not throw the match on the floor. You can trust me. Give me a match!'

'Do you promise?'

'Yes, I promise,' Joseph said, his face a picture of charm.

I handed him a match, let him light his own cigar and watched him take a long puff.

'Thank you,' he said, looking me straight in the eye while simultaneously throwing the lit match on the floor.

'Hey!' I said, stamping out the flame. 'You promised you wouldn't do that!'

'I lied,' Joseph said, before turning on his downtrodden heel and swaggering off down the corridor.

I felt a bit foolish for falling for his patter that day, although I got off very lightly compared to some other people. Several years later, when I was working on Ward 14, I heard that Joseph had somehow managed during one of his stays to book a Rolls Royce that, unbelievably, came to collect him from the front of the hospital. He then had the gall to check into the town's most expensive hotel, where he lived the high life for several days, nobody realising he didn't have a penny to his name until his mood crashed. 'Can you phone the mental hospital and ask them to come and get me?' he asked the gobsmacked manager. 'I'm on Ward 40. They know me very well.'

Philomena was an elderly lady who talked frequently about how she had travelled the world and visited America. She had been in the hospital for decades and was chronically institutionalised, though her detailed descriptions of the sweet taste of the coconut milk she drank fresh from the trees in Barbados, not to mention the magnificent sunset she saw over the Golden Gate Bridge, were extremely convincing.

'Tell me about your travels,' I'd say.

When she was in the mood all sorts of memories would flow, of climbing to the top of the Eiffel Tower, seeing a sell-out show on Broadway or sailing on a paddle steamer in Mississippi, a word she was proud to know how to spell and would repeat to me as we'd been taught at school: 'M.i.s.s.i.s.s.i.p.p.i'. Whatever experience she described, Philomena always shared it with the same conviction, so much so that I wondered if there was at least some truth in her stories. Perhaps she'd made some trips abroad as a child or a young woman?

'Did you really go there?' I'd ask. 'It sounds wonderful. How did you get there? Were you young when you went there?'

This was generally the point where Philomena clamped her lips together and decided she didn't want to do any more talking, and when I usually told myself not to be so daft as to fall for her tall tales.

It wasn't easy to get to know Philomena, especially for the male nurses, because she seemed to have a deep-rooted hatred of all men. On a bad day she would slap the more inexperienced male nursing assistants, and at mealtimes she had a habit of throwing her food or suddenly jumping up and swiping the dinner plates onto the floor, especially when the male staff were around. In time I learned that she only ever spoke to those who persisted in trying to get to know her and put in the hours making an effort, regardless of how little she gave back.

Jonathan and I both got to know Philomena very well in the end, although it inevitably took Jonathan a lot longer than it did me. 'How are you today?' he'd ask, but Philomena would just ignore him and rub her hands together as if she were cold, a sign that she was getting irritated. 'Go away, go away,' she always said to him. It was years before Philomena deigned to say, 'Hello, Jonathan,' and many years more before she started to give him a kiss on the cheek, a sight I always found very touching. We'd both known her for at least a decade by the time this happened and we had come to love her dearly, visiting her regularly in the care home she was eventually moved to.

On one of these visits Philomena mentioned that she'd travelled the world and visited America, something she hadn't spoken about in quite some time.

'Did you fly to America, Philomena?' I asked.

'No,' she replied. 'I didn't fly.'

'Did you go by boat?'

'No.'

'Oh! So how did you get there?'

I thought she might end the conversation there, as she had done many times before, but that's not what happened. This time, Philomena paused and gave me the biggest smile, one that lit up her whole face.

'I went by catapult!' she announced with a flourish.

Philomena had relatives who never once came to see her, and on her death they took what little money she had and refused to pay for a headstone, leaving her to be buried in an unmarked grave. Jonathan and I were so upset about this. We were all too familiar with the historic stories of the many patients who were buried in unmarked graves in the rough ground behind the hospital. This practice had stopped long before we worked there, although the hospital still had a long way to go in terms of treating the deceased with dignity. I remember that a notice of death would be sent to a relative or next of kin, the last line of which read: 'If it is your intention to remove the body for interment and provide the coffin, please inform me by return of post, otherwise arrangements will be made with the Union Authorities.' This was still happening up until the late 1980s, and I recall one such notice being sent to the husband of a thirty-year-old woman.

In the main it wasn't customary for nurses to attend patients' funerals, particularly in the early days of my career, and many had miserable ceremonies with only officials in attendance, and no flowers or words from loved ones. However, nothing would have stopped Jonathan and me from saying our goodbyes to Philomena.

My mother had shown me that sometimes, as a nurse, you form such a deep connection with your patients that your feelings for them transcend all etiquette and tradition. I can remember that when I was a young teenager my mother started bringing one of her patients to our house for Christmas lunch. Edith was a very intelligent woman and knew exactly what sort of hospital she was in, and Mum felt really sorry for her, always saying that the least she could do was give her a taste of normality at Christmastime. The first time I met Edith I couldn't take my eyes off her. She had a prosthetic arm that was huge and completely out of scale with the rest of her body, the fingers painted with bright-pink chipped nail varnish. Our dog was equally fascinated and spent the entire day obsessed with licking poor Edith's arm. At fourteen I didn't understand why Mum had chosen to invite this particular patient out of all the hundreds of men and women she nursed, but when I look back now, of course I understand: nobody can legislate for the human relationships we form as nurses.

To this day, Jonathan and I still visit Philomena's grave, keeping it tidy and laying flowers. And whenever I'm there I never fail to look up to the sky and think about our lovely Philomena, catapulting across the Atlantic and travelling the world from her hospital ward, a big grin stretched across her face.

After working at the same hospital for more than six years, at last I was a registered mental health nurse. To say I was as pleased as Punch is an understatement; I was absolutely *delighted* with myself.

'Hello, Staff Nurse Gibson,' I said gleefully whenever the phone rang on Ward 14 the day I qualified. 'How can I help?'

'It's me.'

'Oh, hi, Mum, are you OK?'

'Yes, love, I'm fine. I only called because you asked me to!'

I laughed and thanked her for phoning, adding, 'Feel free to call again, any time!'

I was so proud to have become a qualified nurse that I just had to hear myself say those words. *Staff Nurse Gibson*. Who'd have thought I'd make it this far? Not seventeen-year-old me, that's for sure.

The patients on Ward 14 were invariably considered too dangerous or untrustworthy to be allowed to go on any of the annual excursions to North Wales, and nobody I worked with could recall the last time a group outing had taken place beyond the grounds of the hospital. Along with a couple of other qualified staff nurses, I decided it was high time we put this right and arranged a Ward 14 outing.

Kirsty, a patient I was very fond of, had put the idea in my head when we were watching TV together one day. *Wish You Were Here . . . ?* was on and Judith Chalmers was reporting from a Mediterranean beach. 'I've never seen the sea,' Kirsty said matter-of-factly. 'I'd like to, though.'

I couldn't believe it, my mind flicking back to those countless trips I'd made to Butlin's as a child, and so many visits to the coast since then. Kirsty was quite a few years older than me and this was unacceptable – I was going to sort it out.

It was easier said than done, I discovered. In the coming weeks I learned that organising a group outing beyond the grounds of the hospital required multiple layers of authorisation, including special permission from senior management. We also had to have at least one member of staff per patient, and of course not all patients would be given permission by their care team to leave the ward.

When we finally got the green light after three or four weeks of planning and crossing our fingers, I was cock-a-hoop. Nine out of our fifteen patients were allowed on the trip, and along with Kirsty we had Nikolajs, Rex, Benedict, Marie, Ralph and Stuart. A gentle, vulnerable young woman called Melissa was also joining us, as well as an older gentleman called Leonard who had been diagnosed with schizophrenia as a young man but was now starting to 'burn out', his symptoms diminishing with age.

There were several resorts we could reach in order to have three or four hours by the sea and return the same day on the hospital bus, and as the self-appointed organiser-in-chief I thought it would be nice if we asked the patients themselves where they wanted to go. My friends Sally and Kim had volunteered to come along. Both were also newly qualified nurses and full of youthful optimism, and they agreed that it was a great idea to empower the patients in the decision-making process. 'It'll really help everyone look forward to it,' Kim said. 'Let's put it to the vote!'

Gayle had been sitting in the corner of the dining room doing her crossword, but having overheard our conversation she put down her pencil and looked over the top of her reading glasses.

'If I were you,' she said diplomatically, 'I'd go somewhere small and quiet, and go midweek. And *you* decide.'

I might have had the letters RMN after my name, but I was still learning from the more experienced nurses every day, and happy to do so.

'Oh yes, Gayle,' I said, realising she was quite right – if we asked the patients it could be 1990 before they all agreed on a plan, and who knows where we'd end up? 'I'm just so pleased this is happening,' I said. 'And I want it all to be really good!'

We settled on a genteel resort known for its golden sands and Victorian tea rooms, and we would go on a Wednesday, since none of the nurses who put their names down fancied a long bus trip the morning after a Monday night at Benny's.

Agatha and four other patients were deemed too violent or dangerous to leave the ward at that time and had to stay behind, but the plan was that they would have a picnic outside if the weather stayed dry. Only Seth refused to come on the trip or indeed take part in any other 'frivolities' on offer. 'I'll be glad o' the peace 'n' quiet,' he said, which made me feel very sorry for the staff left behind on the ward with him.

On the day of the outing Seth was saying the same thing all over again, loudly, and to anyone who would listen. 'You, woman,' he said to me. 'When are ye goin'? When will I 'ave me peace 'n' quiet?'

'Not long now!' I sang, enjoying the buzz on the ward. There were a lot more staff than patients milling about and the day trippers had got up earlier than usual and were already washed,

dressed – some in their bundles, others in their own clothes –
and eating breakfast. Not only that, the early-morning sun was
chiselling through the dirty Perspex windows, giving a grainy
glimpse of the promise of the day ahead.

'Where's Kirsty?' I asked, looking around the dining room.

Kirsty had been beside herself with excitement for weeks, asking
me all sorts of questions about the resort, what we would do when
we got there and whether she could paddle in the sea.

'Of course you can paddle in the sea! And we can walk on the
sand, have a go on the coconut shy, go to the cafe. There's loads
to do, you'll love it.'

'Candyfloss? Can we get candyfloss, Belinda?'

'I'm sure we can.'

Sally appeared at my side. 'Kirsty woke up in a very bad mood,'
she said, pulling a face. 'Nicola is with her in the lounge. Talking
her down, hopefully.'

As well as having a winning way with our pub singer Victor,
our petite nurse Nicola had also developed a great relationship
with Kirsty, so much so that if Nicola ever came into work a little
bit hungover, she'd ask Kirsty to move over in her bed so she
could have a lie-down next to her. It was a little bit strange, even
in those more tolerant and less 'professional' days, but even so
nobody really batted an eyelid. When a nurse managed to develop
a strong therapeutic relationship with a patient it was always to be
applauded, and we'd been grateful to Nicola on many occasions
when Kirsty had a psychotic episode and needed calming down.

Time was moving on and there was still no sign of Kirsty or Nicola. 'I'll go back and see what's going on,' Sally said. 'I'm sure it'll be fine.'

I desperately didn't want to leave Kirsty behind but this did not bode well, and when Sally returned to the dining room she was pulling an even worse face than before. 'She's not good,' she hissed. 'Not good at all.'

It seemed that Kirsty's mental health had started to deteriorate quite dramatically that morning and she was having the same delusions we'd seen many times before, yelling 'Stop fucking looking at me!' at anybody and everybody and nobody in particular. By now the bus was standing on the drive at the front of the hospital and the other patients were starting to line up in the corridor. If we didn't get going on schedule we'd lose some of our precious few hours by the sea. There was clearly only one thing for it, and after a swift committee meeting of the assembled nurses we decided Kirsty would have to be given a dose of droperidol, a liquid anti-psychotic that was commonly used at the time. Droperidol also has a sedative effect and usually works rapidly, so the hope was that if we gave Kirsty a dose now she would calm down on the bus, her delusions would fade and by the time we arrived at the seaside she'd be stable, and we'd all be able to enjoy the day. This was the best-case scenario, of course, and we all knew there was a risk the plan might not work the way we wanted it to. But this trip had come about because of Kirsty, nobody wanted her to miss out and we were all prepared to take the chance. Besides, our secret weapon Nicola was coming on the outing and we had a total of nine members of staff on board. Whatever happened, we would deal with it – it was our job to get on and deal with it.

As the bus set off down the hospital's long driveway, fury was sparkling in Kirsty's eyes and she was turning the air blue. Nicola and a male nurse were flanking her on the back seat, but she was fighting against them and threatening to kill 'you', whoever 'you' was. It was decided that until the droperidol took effect, it would be safer for everyone if Kirsty was restrained, and two male nurses did this by taking an arm each and holding it in a locked position so Kirsty had to stay still and couldn't easily hit anyone.

It took almost an hour before the droperidol eventually started to calm her down, though Kirsty continued to shout out delusional thoughts sporadically throughout the journey. My professional instinct was telling me this was not going to end well, but despite the shiny new letters after my name this was a labour of love, and my heart was winning the day.

She's going to love it when we get there. She'll forget about everything else when she sees the sea.

The journey passed quickly. I thought how it must have been quite overwhelming for the patients of the harshly lit, Dettol-infused Ward 14 to be heading to the coast, bright yellow sunlight dancing on the windows of the bus and the smell of cut grass and hot diesel wafting through the open windows. Still, they were generally being very calm, none of the other patients paying any attention to Kirsty's random outbursts from the back seat or making any trouble themselves.

Ralph was sitting at the front behind the driver, singing along to the tunes on the radio and trying to look cool and aloof in a cloud of Benson & Hedges, though nobody was really giving him a second look either. All the other patients and most of the staff were also smoking to their hearts' content, stubbing out fag ends in the little metal ashtrays attached to the back of the seat in front.

Jack was one of the nurses on the trip. He had a great sense of humour, enjoyed a good gossip and loved to have a story to tell – just as well, as Jack was the nurse we accidentally sedated years earlier, injecting him through the leg of his trousers.

'Daft sod,' I heard him say to another nurse. 'What was he thinking?'

A passing fire engine had sparked a conversation about a spate of fires we'd had all around the hospital recently. My ears pricked up; this had been a source of great intrigue because nobody knew why such an unprecedented number of fires had started to break out. The hospital had had its own small fire station for many years, a throwback to another age when making the hospital self-sufficient and keeping the patients segregated from the rest of society was considered a high priority. The fire station had been subsidised by the government for as long as anyone could remember and was not as unusual as it might sound – ours was not the only large-scale psychiatric hospital that had its own fire station.

The men who ran the service were volunteers from the nursing staff, giving their time for free unless they were called out to tackle a blaze, in which case they received a small payment. There had been so many fires lately that the staff had begun to jokingly suggest the volunteers must be starting fires on purpose to pocket a few quid. I laughed when I heard that. As if a nurse would start a fire in their own hospital!

'Who's a daft sod?' I asked Jack. 'What's happened?'

Jack couldn't keep his face straight when he told me the story. Unbelievably, the last time the fire alarm went off the nurse volunteer in question jumped in the fire engine and raced off to tackle the blaze in record time. The trouble was, he did so without asking a single question, not even about where the fire had started within our extremely large hospital, multiple outbuildings and sprawling acres of grounds. And while the other volunteers were still scratching their heads, our hapless hero was already pulling out his fireman's hose and putting out the small flames, conveniently located inside a bin in a remote and disused farm building, thus giving himself away.

'Talk about caught red-handed!' someone said and we all laughed. It turned out the same nurse had been responsible for every one of the recent fires, but even so, when I heard that he had been sacked I did feel a bit sorry for him, as did Sally. We all made mistakes – Sally and I certainly had – though we had to concede that committing arson on multiple occasions at the hospital was rather more serious than any of our foolish misdemeanours.

Kirsty was very quiet when we parked up at the resort and she walked calmly off the bus, linking arms only with Nicola.

'We'll see you back here in four hours,' we told the driver.

'Right you are,' he said, giving a jaunty thumbs-up to the eclectic group of patients assembled on the pavement. 'Have fun, and mind you all behave yourselves!'

The patients stared back at him while a pensioner walking past with his dog looked over in our direction. None of the staff were in uniform and I don't think the man was looking at us in anything but a casual way. It was just an innocuous glance, but Kirsty took exception to it.

'What you fucking looking at?' she screamed, making the man jump out of his skin. 'I'm gonna fucking kill you!'

Several of the nurses started offering profuse apologies and Nicola immediately tried to steer Kirsty away from the group. The man hurried off, shaking his head, but Kirsty refused to budge, standing rooted to the spot and now glowering at all the other patients and staff.

'What you fucking looking at!' she screamed at no one in particular.

Nicola decided that the rest of us were irritating Kirsty and she would be better off being separated slightly from the group.

'Let's start our walk,' Nicola said authoritatively. 'Come on, Kirsty, me and you will lead the way.'

This somehow did the trick and I watched in admiration as Nicola started to lead Kirsty along the prom, several paces ahead of the rest of us. They made quite a comical pair, Kirsty striding purposefully on her long, sturdy legs while little Nicola was almost having to break into a run to keep up. I found myself smiling with relief. *Thank God for that.* Nicola was such a dedicated nurse, one who always went the extra mile with her patients, and a reward like this was painstakingly earned.

I have no idea what happened in the seconds between me having those positive thoughts and then suddenly staring in disbelief at the scene that unravelled before us. 'Stop it!' I shouted in unison with half a dozen colleagues who all rushed to restrain Kirsty. 'Put her down!'

Unfortunately, Nicola's screams were louder than the rest of ours put together. Kirsty had grabbed Nicola's long hair and was spinning her round like a teacup on the fairground, her dainty feet bouncing up and down across the paving stones. It took the collective effort of every member of staff to free Nicola's hair from Kirsty's iron grip, put our shocked colleague back on solid ground and restrain Kirsty, which we did by bringing her down onto the pavement and having four of us sit on top of her.

'Drink this!' Kim ordered, thrusting a medicine pot containing droperidol under Kirsty's nose. Sticking to the prescribed limit was not an option at this stage; we'd ask a doctor to write it up at a later date – provided we could get Kirsty to drink it, that was. The first pot was cast to one side, and then the next, Kirsty spitting out expletives as we tried to cajole, order and bribe her into drinking the medication. It took almost half an hour to get her to take it and for her to be calm again, all manner of seaside delights having been promised, including a turn on the coconut shy.

It had been a terrible start but we'd come this far. Things could only get better, surely? Nicola was trying to be optimistic too. She brushed herself down and fixed her black hair into a fresh ponytail, unable to conceal a wince as she did so. 'I'm fine,' she said. 'It'll all be OK now. Come on, Kirsty.' This time Nicola made sure she had a large male nurse linking Kirsty's other arm and the three of them began walking down the prom like a mismatched team of three-legged racers.

The other patients were fed up and agitated by now, Ralph complaining about this 'shit day', Marie hiding inside an over-sized hoodie despite the heat, scratching at scabs on her hands and asking if she could go and wait on the coach, and Benedict chewing feverishly on an invisible lump of seaside rock, repeating that he wanted ice cream. The other patients were either wide-eyed, pacing, muttering to themselves or fidgeting anxiously with their clothes.

'Look!' Melissa said suddenly, pointing down the prom. 'Did you see him?'

'Who?' I asked.

'Michael Jackson.'

'No, I must have missed him.'

'Well, he was just there, Belinda,' she assured me, sucking on a strand of her hair and gazing at the horizon.

We carried on, managing to walk the full length of the prom-enade without further incident, most of the patients quietly admiring the view and happily breathing in the sea air. When we reached the far end of the prom we told Kirsty we were close to the coconut shy.

'That's great, isn't it?' Nicola said. 'Aren't we lucky it's open already?'

'I'm gonna fucking kill you!' Kirsty suddenly screamed, eyes flashing from sea to shore as she looked for whoever it was who was terrorising her. Seconds later, to a communal cry of, 'No, Kirsty!' I watched in horror as she leapt over the blue-painted metal railings that ran the length of the promenade, clearing the top rail like a champion hurdler. A little red Mini was parked in a bay on the other side, facing out towards the sea, and inside the car were an elderly couple who were enjoying their lunch, parcels of fish and chips open on their laps and mugs of tea balanced in between them.

'I'm gonna fucking kill you! What are you fucking looking at?'

'No, Kirsty! No!'

As six or seven nurses – myself included – started scrambling up and over the railings, Kirsty began lifting up the side of the car and rocking it backwards and forwards. She was as strong as an ox and the terrified old couple screamed as they were tossed about like dinghies in a choppy sea, fish and chips and hot tea spilling everywhere. My colleagues and I attached ourselves to Kirsty like magnets, desperate to restrain her, but even mob-handed it wasn't easy. Kirsty's hands were like a pair of vices, clamped tightly to the chassis of the Mini, and in the end the only way we could make her let go was by pulling as hard as we could, a chain of nurses heaving in unison like a practising tug-of-war team.

Once Kirsty was prostrate on the promenade, Sally and I sat on her legs, Nicola perched on her chest and several other nurses held down her arms and her head, which was resting on a towel we'd brought for the beach. Holding her still was a monumental effort; Kirsty was fighting against us with all her might and continuing to shout, 'I'm gonna kill you,' which she directed at every passer-by who dared cast their eyes in our direction, as well as those who looked the other way and tried to pretend they hadn't seen us.

Placating the elderly couple was not an easy task, requiring every ounce of charm and diplomacy we could muster.

'She tossed my vehicle around as if it were a Tonka toy!' the gentleman said, still clearly very shocked. 'My wife is traumatised. Our lunch is ruined, not to mention our clothes, and the car.'

His beige slacks were splattered with tea and his wife was shakily removing the remains of their lunch from the car, turfing fish and chips from the seats and the floor mats into the gutter. The overexcited flock of seagulls that descended on her was the last thing she needed. 'Shoo, shoo!' she said uselessly, the birds squawking and flapping their wings in pleasure at this unexpected banquet.

'We should report this to the police!' the man said in disgust.

By now it was only too obvious that our patients came from a psychiatric hospital, and that all the nurses were having a tough time, but I still had a lot of sympathy for the couple – they'd been through an ordeal they were unlikely ever to forget. We managed to make peace with them eventually, two fresh portions of fish and chips, complete with bread rolls and mushy peas, going a long way in securing the truce.

At this juncture the sensible thing would have been to call it a day before anything else went wrong, but we still had eight other patients besides Kirsty to think about, and we'd come this far, in every sense. Once again we decided by committee that keeping Kirsty topped up with medication was the only way forward, and Nicola poured another large dose of droperidol into a can of fizzy drink.

'Drink this, please,' Nicola told her. 'All of it.' Kirsty began to gulp the can of Lilt down greedily, a sight that I think settled the nerves of all the staff.

'Let's go to the coconut shy,' Jack said. 'She's been looking forward to that. And those blokes look like they can handle themselves if she kicks off!'

I followed his gaze. 'Very droll,' I smiled, looking at the two young lads who were running the stall, both as thin as lollipop sticks. I appreciated Jack's positive attitude. A couple of the other nurses were starting to look weary and lose patience, I think, but we all needed to keep our energy high and our sense of humour intact.

This time, before we moved a muscle, we put a military plan in place, deciding who was going to flank Kirsty and exactly how we'd react if she had another episode.

'Right then, let's go and have some fun!' Sally said, chivvying the other patients down a boardwalk that led onto the beach.

'Look!' Melissa exclaimed excitedly. 'Did you see him?'

For once I was glad of the question. At least one of the patients was engaging with us instead of looking bored, poker-faced or irritated.

'Who?' a few of the staff gamely asked.

'Stevie Wonder. He was just there!'

'No! What a shame we missed him. Do you think he was going to meet Michael Jackson?'

Melissa shrugged, a look of wonderment on her face. 'I suppose so.'

I pushed on a few paces ahead to pay the stallholders at the coconut shy. Kirsty would have the first turn, we had decided, which we hoped would please her. We also thought this was something she could potentially be very good at, given that she clearly had the strength of a professional shot-putter.

One of the young lads walked to the front of the stall as I approached, a welcoming smile on his face, but just at that moment Kirsty's half-drunk can of Lilt flew past both of us and hit his friend on the back.

'What the fuck?' the lad shouted, looking round in shock.

'I'm so, so sorry,' I said.

Meanwhile, Kirsty had managed to break free from my colleagues and was not only sprinting away from the group at breakneck speed, but zoning in on a big box of coconuts lying at the side of the stall. She managed to lob several in all directions – thankfully without hitting anyone else – before we managed to wrestle her to the ground yet again.

'What are you fucking looking at?' she shouted, eyes scanning the clouds as she lay pinned into the sand.

'This is beyond a joke,' one of my less patient colleagues muttered. 'We can't carry on like this.'

Nicola reluctantly said she had to agree. 'I'm sorry, Belinda. I think we need to call back the bus driver earlier than planned.'

At least we'd set foot on the beach, I thought. All was not lost, and at the ripe old age of twenty-eight Kirsty could finally say she'd been to the seaside.

The other patients were slowly deteriorating in different ways by this time, red flags waving more noticeably over some than others. Leonard had a habit of scratching his head, and while he'd been standing around he'd opened up some scabs on his bald scalp, making them bleed. He had also started going up to passing strangers and attempting to introduce himself. Not only did he look very intimidating – he was an enormous man, with hands like shovels – but we knew from experience that if you shook hands with Leonard he would squeeze yours so hard it cut off your circulation. I saw a young man pull his wife away in fear as Leonard approached with an outstretched hand and blood oozing on top of his head; it was definitely time to make a move.

We told the patients we were going to wait in the cafe over the road until the bus driver was ready to collect us, which none of them questioned. Benedict was salivating at the prospect of having an ice cream *and* a doughnut, and though Nikolajs was looking more impatient than I'd ever seen him, he made a point of saying, 'Thank you, thank you.' When we got inside the cafe he pulled out a chair for me. 'Belinda, please,' he said, gesturing to the seat like a flamboyant butler.

I'd never been so glad to sit down. I felt like I'd been in the wrestling ring with Big Daddy, as did most of the other nurses. Kirsty also seemed shattered. For such a young woman she always looked tired and worn, years of fighting, violence and medication having taken their toll on her pleasant, open face and pale complexion.

'Here,' Nicola said, 'have a little drink of that.'

There was a collective sigh of relief when this latest medicine pot was taken without argument, swiftly drained and discarded onto the red-and-white gingham tablecloth. We had filled three full tables and taken over half the cafe, and while this was going on the other customers were giving us sideways looks as they no doubt worked out where we were from.

'Are you ready to order?'

The question from the cheerful teenage waitress provoked quite a pantomime.

'I have five sugars in my tea,' Benedict said forcefully. 'Five. I have FIVE sugars in my tea.'

As he started to repeat himself for a third time, and ask for ice cream, all the other patients were loudly talking over each other and several nurses were desperately trying to get them to stop and take turns.

'They won't get me!' Stuart suddenly interjected, his hand readjusting his invisible earpiece. 'Get on to HQ. Tell the commander, IMMEDIATELY.'

'Here you are,' Jack said, giving Stuart a nudge and a wink. 'Have a swig of that, mate.'

Another empty medicine pot rolled into the middle of the tablecloth; at this rate we'd be clean out of PRN medication and the doctors would definitely be complaining about how many prescriptions they'd have to sign off after the event. That thought was still percolating through my brain when Leonard started 'eating' items pictured on the laminated menu card. This was a habit we were very used to. He did it every time he read a magazine or watched TV, 'drinking' cans of pop, 'eating' spaghetti and then wiping the tomato sauce from his chin and 'sipping' mugs of hot coffee and tea. His bizarre behaviour often extended beyond food and drink, and if he saw a picture of a gun he would always start to shoot the staff and patients on the ward. Sometimes I would take the imaginary gun off him and lock it in his room.

'Ahh, don't do that, Belinda,' Leonard would cry.

'I have no choice, Leonard,' I would say. 'We can't have you shooting people.'

Understandably, the young waitress was in quite a tizzy by the time we'd managed to place our order, while the other customers were unable to take their eyes off us, looking like they were enjoying the spectacle from their front-row seats. Some of the older customers gave me and my colleagues well-meaning smiles, and one particularly sweet old lady turned to her companion and said: 'Aren't nurses *marvellous*?'

'Who said that?' Kirsty shrieked, standing bolt upright and

swivelling her head around. 'Who the fuck do you think you are?'

She appeared to be talking to the trays of glasses stacked near the display counter behind the table she was sitting at. They were arranged in school-dinner fashion, one loaded tray of glasses topped with another, the number of glasses descending the higher the stack went. This display was a particularly impressive one, made of six tiers of glass beakers, all neatly positioned and shining under a fluorescent strip light. Catastrophically, in the blink of an eye Kirsty zoned in on the tray at the bottom, grabbing hold of it and throwing the entire display in the air in one fell swoop. It happened so fast I'd barely caught my breath before pieces of broken glass and upturned trays were scattering across the floor, creating a carpet of booby traps between most of the staff and Kirsty.

'You looking at me? Are ya?'

'No, Kirsty!' Nicola cried. 'No! Listen to me, Kirsty, no!'

Nicola dashed at Kirsty like a whippet from a trap, but she was not quick enough.

'D'you want milk with that?' Kirsty said, addressing the kind old lady who had admired the nurses. 'Do you?'

No, no, no! Not this!

Nobody, Nicola included, managed to restrain Kirsty before she liberated one of her breasts from inside her T-shirt and gave it a firm squeeze. The milk that shot from her nipple missed the poor woman's teacup and squirted straight across the tablecloth, splattering into a plate containing two fresh cream buns.

Kirsty was restrained on the back seat of the bus once again, the doses of droperidol finally starting to have the sedative effect we'd been waiting for all day. It was the other anti-psychotic drug she was taking – chlorpromazine – that made Kirsty lactate. It's a distressing side effect for patients to contend with, but Kirsty had clearly found a way of weaponising it to her advantage. We'd seen her pull this stunt before, and unfortunately the last person to be offered milk with his tea had been our long-suffering vicar, who was rudely interrupted when he was trying to enjoy a quiet cuppa during one of his Sunday ward rounds. By the shade of deep scarlet his whole head glowed that day, I think he found this even more embarrassing than Delores's demands for sex in the corridor.

By the time we left the resort, as well as seeing Michael Jackson and Stevie Wonder, Melissa had also spotted Elvis Presley, John Lennon and Neil Diamond. The excitement must have tired her out because she was nodding off almost as soon as she got on the bus. The same went for several other patients, who fell asleep soon after we left the seaside. As we travelled back along the motorway the rest were happy to sit and smoke, listen to the radio or gaze out of the window, and the journey passed quickly and without incident. Most importantly, Kirsty stayed calm and silent, and when we weren't very far from the hospital Jack gamely suggested we stop at a pub.

'I think we've all earned a drink,' he said. 'Let's go to the King's Head.'

After a very short discussion about whether or not this was a good idea – shouldn't we really be cutting our losses and getting back to the ward after the day we'd had? – the staff unanimously voted to visit the pub. Our trip to the sea had been cut short, after all, and so why not? None of the patients objected, and our happy-go-lucky driver said he knew a scenic route that would take us to the King's Head in no time. A pint of Holsten Pils and a Southern Comfort chaser was exactly what I needed, I thought, picturing the sunny garden of this well-known local hostelry.

Not long to wait now.

We were within touching distance of the village when Stuart suddenly leapt to his feet. 'We can't go this way!' he shouted. 'Driver, turn around and go back over the bridge!' He said this with great authority, his hand shooting to his invisible earpiece. Jack was sitting beside him, and he immediately started trying to talk Stuart round, reassuring him there was nothing to worry about.

'There is a VERY GREAT DEAL to be worried about,' Stuart said dramatically. 'Jim Maguire is waiting for me, he's going to get me! Stop the bus! We have to turn around.'

The driver looked back over his shoulder and held up his left palm. 'What's it to be?'

'Do a left here, mate,' Jack sighed, telling Stuart to sit down, and that all would be well as we would go on a different route and didn't need to cross the bridge.

Our driver wasn't at all bothered and said he knew another way to get to the pub, but as soon as we started to approach the village from the other side Stuart was on his feet and flapping all over again.

'He's here. They'll kill me! Turn around!'

As much as we all liked this particular pub, Stuart was obviously very rattled about its location and it was not worth this amount of hassle. We asked the driver to forget about the King's Head, get us back en route to the hospital and stop at the next pub that looked half-decent. Stuart was pacified by this and sat quietly for all of five minutes before jumping up again when we reached a large crossroads and the driver indicated right.

'Stop! You can't go that way, Jim Maguire's men are all over this town!'

The driver's upturned palm was back, and once again we made a detour and headed in another direction. The same thing happened twice more, Jim Maguire and his men seemingly criss-crossing the county and popping up in every village within a twenty-mile radius of the hospital. The other patients were getting visibly twitchy and Kirsty was sitting bolt upright in her seat, eyes starting to flash. Meanwhile Jack was gagging for a drink and losing patience. 'Stuart!' he implored. 'Nobody is going to get you. You're safe with us. If you just let us carry on and get to the pub, you will see that Jim Maguire is not there, and we can all have a nice time.'

This was not what Stuart wanted to hear and only made him more terrified. 'No! He's going to get me! He'll kill me!' With that Stuart bolted for the door, trying to pull up the lever and open it as we headed along a busy road. It was at that point that we agreed to admit defeat, yet again, and settle on having a drink back at the hospital pub, after our shift.

'Today's been one disaster after another, and that just puts the tin hat on it,' Jack said, looking like he didn't know whether to laugh or cry. 'All I wanted was a pint! Is that too much to ask?'

'Look on the bright side,' Sally said.

'Is there one?'

'Well, it could have been worse, I suppose.'

'How?'

'At least it wasn't as bad as Prestatyn!'

This comment brought a ripple of laughter from the nurses. Though that notorious Prestatyn trip had happened long before my time – somewhere deep in the 1970s – I knew exactly what Sally was referring to. All the staff had heard the story before, but it still made us laugh every time.

'We've had a lovely time in Prestatyn but we must be going now,' the nurse had said, cajoling the elderly man into his seat. 'Come on, now. Chop chop!'

Like a lot of the patients, this frail old boy was discombobulated and disorientated, the culture shock of breathing Welsh sea air for a week after years inside the asylum no doubt taking its toll. There were no seat belts on the coach (we didn't have them until the turn of the century) and this patient had already made several bolts for the door, though luckily not while the coach was moving, as Stuart had just done.

'No, no,' he protested. 'I want to get off. I want to stay here!'

Running out of time and patience, the flustered nurse told him if he didn't behave she'd have to 'take action' because the coach was already late and they had to get going.

'No,' he repeated. 'Please let me off. You have to leave me here.'

'Really,' she said. 'If this behaviour continues, I will have to medicate you. And the next time we organise a trip you won't be coming. You'll have to stay in the hospital.'

That did the trick, and the poor man didn't utter another word for hours on end. However, as soon as the coach pulled up outside the hospital he suddenly became very agitated again, jumping up and asking where he was.

'We're back at the hospital. Where do you think you are?'

'Hospital? But you said if I behaved myself I wouldn't have to go to hospital.'

Even then the penny didn't drop. It was only when the nurse in charge of the trip counted the patients off the bus and discovered that she had more than she started with, that the truth dawned. There was only one explanation, of course: the protesting and 'misbehaving' passenger was not a patient at all, but an unfortunate member of the public who was effectively kidnapped on Prestatyn prom.

'I wonder what happened afterwards?' one of my colleagues mused as we all enjoyed the retelling of the tale.

I think we could guess at the answer to that. Any fallout from the misadventure was never part of the story, because in those days the mistake would have been dealt with as swiftly and discreetly as possible, with apologies and warnings rather than legal action and sackings. And that was precisely the approach we took after our black comedy of errors today. After having said how terribly sorry we were to all offended parties, paid for the smashed glasses and appealed to the sweet nature of the old lady in the cafe, we returned to the hospital safe in the knowledge that what happened at the seaside would stay at the seaside.

'*Kirsty was escorted on a long-planned trip to the seaside,*' Nicola wrote in the log. '*Prior to the trip Kirsty was disturbed and voicing hallucinations and delusions. However, she settled quickly with droperidol as expected on the way to the seaside. Unfortunately this did not have the long-term expected effect and Kirsty became very unsettled and made assaults on staff requiring restraint. She also smashed glasses in a cafe and shook a car with some elderly people in it. No injury suffered to the elderly people although re-assurance was provided. On return to the hospital Kirsty was settled and remains so.*'

Like many patients, Kirsty had started to develop psychotic symptoms as a teenager – I saw a lot of men and women who first showed signs at seventeen, eighteen and nineteen – and in her case she was diagnosed with paranoid schizophrenia at the age of twenty. After committing a series of serious assaults and displaying extremely disturbed behaviour, Kirsty had been locked in a high-security hospital for several years before being down-graded to Ward 14. Unfortunately, not long after her admission to us, Kirsty had broken a nurse's nose by kicking her in the face. As embarrassing, disruptive and alarming as her behaviour had been at the seaside today, a few upset day trippers and stallholders and some smashed glassware were not going to evoke any questions from our superiors. No more was ever said about our calamitous awayday, but it was the last group day trip ever organised for Ward 14, none of the nurses ever daring to organise another in the three remaining years before the hospital shut down. No wonder the patients of Ward 14 were never taken to Prestatyn. Now I knew exactly why.

I still never had any regrets about any of the trips I was involved in, because whatever went wrong there was always a silver lining. At least the patients experienced *something* other than hospital life, and it was surprising what they talked about afterwards. In time, Kirsty reminisced fondly about the softness of the sand as she lay on the beach, the fact that she was restrained while she did so not seeming to bother her one bit, or register at all.

Lena, incidentally, continued the tradition of building her shrine to Val Doonican right up until her death in the early 1990s. I had not seen her for many years when she passed away, though a colleague told me that the ticket from our fateful night out always took pride of place in her room, and she often talked fondly about the night she met 'the only star'.

Lena also continued to play 'If I Knew Then What I Know Now' every morning while she built the shrine. Needless to say, I cannot listen to that song, or 'Walk Tall', without thinking of taking Lena to the concert, or indeed about any of the other ill-fated outings in which I was involved.

CHAPTER 7

'Feelings have to come out somehow'

'It's like being at the bottom of a big, black hole with no way out,' Claudia told me. 'Eventually you stop trying to escape it, and instead you sit it out.'

Claudia was in her twenties, and had been suffering with depression throughout her adult life. I know it's more acceptable nowadays to talk about 'living with' or 'experiencing' depression but I think those words take away the absolute awfulness of depression – and Claudia did suffer, terribly. When she was in her 'sitting it out' phase she entered a state of complete psychomotor retardation, meaning she would need to be washed and dressed and fed by nurses while she mutely allowed this to happen. It's so sad to say it, but at those times she was no more responsive than a lobotomised patient like Ernie, despite the fact that when she was well she was a bright, independent and very intelligent young woman.

There was never any telling how long it would take for Claudia's mood to shift, but gradually the black hole would start to be filled. 'Then you can begin to scramble out,' she told me, 'although sometimes you start slipping back in and you have to start the climb again.'

Since the age of sixteen Claudia had made numerous attempts to hang herself, suffocate herself with a plastic bag and overdose on prescription drugs. Like Sam, she was parasuicidal rather than suicidal, each attempt staged in such a way that she would be discovered and saved before it was too late. When her depression was lifting Claudia's motivation to self-harm increased, although once she had fully climbed out of the darkness she could be perfectly well for months and sometimes even a year or more before her old feelings of not really enjoying life inevitably returned and started to pull her down once again.

In her late teens Claudia had been diagnosed with 'endogenous depression', something that today would more likely be described as a 'mood disorder' or 'major depressive disorder'. Endogenous depression is a severe mental health diagnosis, the depression occurring when there appears to be no external cause and there has been no identifiable trauma or stress that could have triggered it. As Claudia knew all too well, sufferers are unable to experience joy and pleasure and they have overwhelming feelings of sadness, worthlessness and guilt. There are also changes in energy levels, and their whole world seems a sad, dark and lonely place, exactly as Claudia described it.

There is a view that endogenous depression is caused by biological factors, and Claudia's many friends (and I came to count myself in that number) thought there must be some truth in this. After all, on the surface she had everything going for her. Claudia was not a patient on Ward 14, but a fellow nurse, with a great network of support around her. Whenever she was hospitalised she was treated in other hospitals, our superiors always showing her kindness and giving her whatever time off she needed, while keeping her job open for her. Claudia also owned her own flat and had a family who appeared to do all they could to help her.

Unfortunately, to compound her problems, when she was in her late twenties Claudia started to drink heavily. 'It's just a temporary means of escape,' she told me one day when we were sitting in the TV lounge, having a cup of coffee at the end of our shift.

'What is it you're escaping from?' I asked.

'Pressure,' she said without skipping a beat.

'What makes you feel under pressure?'

'Not my illness,' she replied, again without hesitation.

'What, then?'

This question made Claudia think for a few moments.

'The pressure of work, mostly, and the pressure of just *living*,' she said.

Claudia described feeling conflicted and trapped by her job, which she enjoyed and struggled with in equal measure. 'It's hard, isn't it?' she said. 'Knowing you have to keep picking yourself up and keep going. Knowing you have your mortgage to pay.

Wondering what else you would do if you walked away and said, "I don't need the stress."'

I could identify with this, up to a point. Though I've never experienced depression or even low moods – if anything the opposite is true and all these years on I'm still very much an optimist who sees the glass as half full – I certainly worked in a very stressful environment. And however much pressure I had to contend with at work, not doing my job was unthinkable. In my case, I not only had bills to pay and a roof to keep over my head, but I was tied to my profession because I absolutely loved being a nurse. The pull was powerful and unbreakable, and however tough it got – and sometimes it did get very tough indeed – I couldn't imagine doing anything else.

Though Claudia's drinking started as a temporary means of escape when she was feeling particularly stressed, in time it escalated into a daily habit, something that was facilitated in no small way by one of her close friends. Astrid was a rather fierce-looking, straight-talking Swedish woman, and she was also a nurse on Ward 14. Astrid's doctrine was that alcohol 'helps to take the edge off the day'. You would probably describe Astrid as a functioning alcoholic nowadays, and Claudia was heading the same way, although her poison was strong lager as opposed to the high-percentage Swedish vodka Astrid favoured.

As Claudia's drinking intensified their mutual dependency on alcohol bound the two women even closer as friends, and whenever she was hospitalised Astrid was Claudia's most frequent visitor. Astrid was at least a decade older than Claudia, and as well as taking on the role of drinking-buddy-in-chief, she mothered Claudia in many ways, always being very proactive in terms of checking in on her at her flat, making sure she was supported each time she returned to work and, on a few occasions, being the person to raise the alarm when Claudia attempted to take her own life.

When the doctors talked to Claudia about her drinking habits, pointing out that excessive alcohol consumption was not helpful to either her physical or mental health, she always gave them the same answer. 'My drinking has nothing to do with my depression. I drink to relieve stress. If I stopped drinking, the depression would still be there.'

Drinking alcohol can offer instant relief after working demanding shifts and being exposed to pressurised situations, and drinking to cope with stress at work is a concept I've become very familiar with over the years. Nurses drink a lot more alcohol (and use more drugs) than the rest of the population and it's estimated* that one in five nurses will develop a substance misuse disorder, a problem that is likely to be greater than figures show due to under-reporting. The statistics don't surprise me at all. Though

---

* http://news.bbc.co.uk/1/hi/health/944503.stm
https://www.independentnurse.co.uk/professional-article/the-suicide-crisis-in-nursing/223994/
https://www.alcoholrehabguide.org/resources/alcoholism-and-medical-professionals/

nurses need to be emotionally strong at work, feelings have to come out somehow. Letting my hair down at Benny's was always a tonic, and was something I looked forward to (and benefited from) every week. My friends and I rarely talked about work once we'd left the hospital for the night, and the general consensus was that having a drink and a laugh together was not just fun, but a very necessary release from the stress and human suffering we dealt with every day on the wards.

Besides enjoying the weekly booze-up at Benny's, smoking was another regular, go-to antidote to stress. My favourite charge nurse, Neil, was perhaps the most reliant of us all on nicotine, something I only realised when he eventually tried to stop smoking and the calm, laid-back man we all knew and loved was replaced by a short-tempered monster, a transformation not unlike that of mild-mannered scientist Dr David Banner into the apoplectic Incredible Hulk.

It was a nightmare for everyone, and after several failed attempts, one January Neil decided he was going to give it a last try by using the newly arrived nicotine patch, prescribed by his GP as they were not yet available over the counter. When a few of us met in the pub for a drink one night, Neil arrived wearing two patches on each arm and chewing nicotine gum like his life depended on it. The pub was filled with smoke, and before Neil had finished his first pint the second-hand fumes were playing havoc with his willpower. He soon cracked, spitting out the gum and lighting a fag, at which point the rest of us released what had been a collectively held breath as our own Dr David Banner returned to the fold.

As well as drinking more than average, nurses are also twice as likely to experience depression when compared to other occupations. There are also significantly higher levels of suicide amongst nurses than within the general population: Sister Kane's death from suicide was therefore sadly not as unusual as it might have seemed. In fact, nurses are four times more likely to commit suicide than people working in any other profession in the UK, and during my career I'm afraid to say I've known more psychiatric nurses who have killed themselves, or attempted to kill themselves, than patients.

More than 30 per cent of nurses who leave the profession cite 'burnout' as their reason for leaving, another statistic that is not an eye-opener to me. A good nurse needs to be affected by sadness, because, as I've mentioned before, if you're untouched by the pain and suffering of patients you are in the wrong job. But as human beings we can only experience so much misery and sadness without it affecting us profoundly. Managing our emotions is therefore a constant balancing act, because nurses can't help anyone if they become too emotionally involved.

The majority of nurses I've worked with have managed to tread this tightrope very well. Of those who struggled or found it impossible, many entered the profession because they had mental health needs themselves and believed they would be ideally placed to help people in a similar position. Sometimes this worked and sometimes it didn't. I knew nurses who over-identified with their patients and were unable to develop a therapeutic relationship, or they found their own mental health declined because of the stress of work. A friend and colleague who fell into this category once locked herself in the bathroom during a night shift. When she eventually let me in I was shocked to see blood dripping down the front of her white uniform. The young nurse – in her twenties like me – had cut her arms in an act of self-harm, the letting of blood, she explained, inducing the release of tension she craved in the midst of a distressing and hectic shift. The relief it brought her was short-lived. In the wake of this incident my friend went through an incredibly tense period as she reconsidered her career choice and ultimately left for a less pressurised job in the community.

Working through the pandemic brought a whole new set of stresses and incidences of burnout for nurses, and I saw that younger members of staff struggled far more than older nurses. In 2020 I was the chief executive of a charity that supported a secure unit for fifteen patients with dementia, and when the first wave of COVID hit, eight of the patients died, all within a very short space of time. The younger staff were far more traumatised by this than the older carers and nurses, who were predominantly female and had been in the job for many years. It wasn't that the older women had become cold and indifferent (although I think nurses in secure care do have a shelf life, because the need to protect ourselves emotionally can lead to compassion fatigue and desensitisation). Rather, I think the older nurses in this unit were generally very emotionally resilient – perhaps naturally so – in addition to being trained from an early age to unquestioningly 'get on with it'. Dealing with the intensity of suffering that COVID brought was unprecedented for all the staff, but it was exclusively the younger nurses who started to leave the job and, in many cases, the profession. The decline in training, supervision, staffing levels, pay and conditions all played their part in the exodus, though research* bears out the fact that younger nurses in particular are leaving the profession because of emotional health: 46 per cent of nurses under twenty-five describe themselves as 'not emotionally healthy', compared to just 19 per cent in the fifty-five-and-over age group.

When I think back to my own experiences, and some of the highly stressful situations I found myself in at a young age, I realise I was emotionally strong enough to survive whatever was thrown at me, and usually without crying (though many times I had to fight back tears). And in hindsight, I think every challenge, however daunting, taught me something about how to be a better nurse.

As a very young nursing assistant the most demanding job I was given was assisting in the electroconvulsive therapy (ECT) suite. It tested my resilience to the limit and remains the most upsetting and emotionally challenging task of my career.

ECT was and still is a form of treatment that divides opinion and is hotly debated within the mental health field. Some people

---

* www.voice.ons.org

argue very strongly that it is a viable and worthwhile treatment for those patients with severe depression who haven't responded to psychological therapy or pharmacology, and it's true that ECT can have a dramatic and positive effect on some. The late actress Carrie Fisher, for example, swore by regular sessions to treat her persistent depression, while others argue that the risk of suffering long-lasting or permanent memory loss, amongst other possible side effects, is too high a price to pay. Ernest Hemingway is reported to have shared this view with his biographer before he committed suicide shortly after being given ECT in 1961: 'Well, what is the sense of ruining my head and erasing my memory, which is my capital, and putting me out of business? It was a brilliant cure but we lost the patient . . .'

There are many theories about exactly how ECT works, yet we still have no definitive answer. The practice involves giving the patient an anaesthetic before sending an electric current through their brain that triggers a brief seizure. In its early days ECT was given unethically, sometimes using larger currents and without consent (as portrayed in *One Flew Over the Cuckoo's Nest*). It can still be given today without consent in some circumstances, though only when mental health professionals have very solid grounds to believe it will be a beneficial therapeutic intervention.

Several months before I was sent to work in the ECT suite I looked after a lady called Noreen who, like Claudia, was so depressed she was diagnosed with psychomotor retardation. Noreen couldn't eat without assistance and had to be fed every day. In the depths of her illness she would remain eerily still and motionless for long periods of time, staring blindly into space for hour after hour. At those times Noreen didn't respond to any interventions at all, and she continued to be in this stupor for weeks.

The decision was taken to give Noreen ECT, and to my surprise the effect was transformative. After just one session she woke from the anaesthetic and started laughing and smiling and saying how well she felt, and within days Noreen went home to her husband. The electrical surge appeared to have somehow reset Noreen's brain, I thought. I was totally bowled over by this mysterious and apparently miraculous cure. 'I had no idea ECT could do this,' I marvelled.

'No,' snorted Beryl, the straight-talking older nurse I worked with back in those early days on the open wards. 'Not a lot of people do, love.'

It didn't take me long to understand why Beryl said this with such a bitter tone in her voice.

The ECT suite was run by Dr Hardy, a terrifying woman with a yellowing silver bob who barked orders at everyone and constantly sniped at the student nurses, calling them stupid morons and idiots. She was equally dismissive of some of the qualified nurses, forbidding those she disliked from working with her or even setting foot inside the ECT suite.

I was incredibly green and very nervous when I first entered the suite, though in the event it was not Dr Hardy who terrified me but the treatment itself. I found it very distressing to watch patients being wheeled in and attached to machines that looked like they belonged in an experimental laboratory rather than an NHS hospital, and the patients themselves looked either scared to death or alarmingly oblivious to what they were letting themselves in for.

Worryingly, Dr Hardy's hands never stopped shaking. I assumed she was nervous and had no control over this, although at the moment when she put the cannula into the patient's hand ready for the anaesthetic she somehow stopped shaking for those vital few seconds, before her hands immediately turned to wobbling blancmanges once again. When the electrical charge ran through the patient's brain and the fit took hold I watched in horror, holding my breath and feeling extremely fearful. A team of nurses held the patient's limbs and head because he was shaking so violently – I would learn that it was not unheard of for patients to physically hurt themselves, or even break bones, while undergoing ECT (though this didn't happen at my hospital). It seemed like such a brutal and archaic treatment, and rather than hoping for another miracle like Noreen's, I found myself praying the poor patient would simply survive undamaged. Afterwards, having been given no training whatsoever, I was sent to provide aftercare in the recovery room as the patient came round from the anaesthetic. He had a Brook airway in his mouth, a device to help keep his windpipe open and his tongue safely out of the way during the treatment. When the patient started coughing, that was the moment I was supposed to remove the plastic device, but nobody had told me this. It meant the poor man just coughed and coughed and eventually pulled it out himself whilst I just sat there not having a bloody clue about what I should or shouldn't be doing. I then walked the thin patient back to his ward. It was far too soon for him to be walking and he bobbed about beside me like a strip of dangling elastic. Looking back on it now, the way I 'cared for' him and other patients in the recovery room that day was inhumane: I was an incompetent teenager and untrained nurse, and it should never have happened. That afternoon, after I'd returned the last of the ECT patients to their different wards, I sat outside on a bench and smoked cigarettes one after the other, reflecting on the complete awfulness of the whole experience both for the patients and for me. I was feeling very sorry for myself, and fortunately I was never sent back to the ECT suite. I couldn't bear the thought of it, and my superiors protected me from it.

In all my years at the hospital I never saw or heard of a patient who benefited from ECT in the remarkable way Noreen did. Nobody even came close. Most patients had a very slight improvement or showed no change at all, and those who did appear to have responded positively always seemed to deteriorate between treatments, which is why patients generally had a lengthy course of ECT rather than just one session like Noreen.

Over the last few decades the use of ECT has dramatically declined, something I am wholly in favour of.

*

The old expression, 'If we didn't laugh we'd cry,' was one that was used a lot on Ward 14. We used humour liberally to deal with the utter sadness and human despair we dealt with every day. The pranks we played on each other often had a dark side to them, but they helped relieve the sadness and tension when times were tough and, ultimately, allowed us to keep calm and carry on.

An elderly long-term patient called Cyril was made a 'trustee' on Ward 14 in the mid-1980s, which meant he was trusted to hold the keys to the kitchen and had controlled access to tea- and coffee-making facilities for both patients and staff. He loved this position and was always up early, already pottering around by the time the day staff had taken over from the night nurses, keen to fetch everyone a morning brew.

Sadly, Cyril was in very poor physical health, and one night he passed away peacefully in his sleep. The night shift had to break the news to the day nurses, which inevitably brought a few jokey remarks along the lines of, 'That's a shame, I'm desperate for a brew!'

One of the nurses on duty had arrived late to changeover that morning, and as a result he missed the handover meeting, and the sad news of Cyril's demise.

'Where's Cyril?' he asked, catching his breath after running down the corridor. 'I could murder a cuppa.'

We all looked at each other sideways, as if to say, 'Who's going to tell him?' before someone piped up, 'Cyril, you say? Oh, he's not up yet, can you go and wake him?'

The wide-eyed male nurse was back minutes later, looking shocked and saddened. 'You're not going to believe this,' he said. 'I hate to tell you, but poor Cyril is dead in his bed.'

Peals of helpless laughter rang out and we all fell about in our seats.

'You bastards!' the nurse shouted before bursting out laughing himself. 'Bloody hell! You got me good and proper there!'

Another memorable prank involved the hospital morgue.

'This is the plan,' a group of young student nurses said to a colleague called Helen. 'You go into the morgue and get on one of the trolleys. Cover yourself up with a sheet, and when the next nurse comes in, jump up and scare the living daylights out of her!'

Helen was game for a laugh and readily agreed to this, anticipating that her friend Bernadette – herself a well-known prankster – would be the next nurse to enter the morgue.

The group of student nurses who set Helen up watched with bated breath as she disappeared inside the imposing wooden entrance doors to the morgue (a place I never entered, by the way – I had no good reason to, and never wanted to).

'We'll give you a minute to hide,' her friends giggled, 'and then we'll switch off the lights.'

'Right,' Helen said, gamely taking herself into the cold-storage room where several other bodies were laid out under sheets.

After the lights were turned out it took less than thirty seconds before Helen was screaming in terror and running back outside, and now it was her turn to shout, 'You bastards!' Hilariously,

Bernadette and the other nurses had turned the tables on Helen, because when Helen took her position under the sheet Bernadette was already on the trolley beside her, hiding under another sheet and trying to hold her breath. When the lights went out, Bernadette wasted no time in leaning across and grabbing hold of Helen's arm, making her jump out of her skin.

'You'd better watch your back!' Helen laughingly warned her friend, once her heart rate had finally returned to normal. 'You won't get away with this!'

All the nurses accepted the deal: if you enjoyed having a giggle at someone else's expense (and we all did), then you also had to suck it up when you were the butt of the joke. And, as I found out on many occasions, it would inevitably be your turn one day.

One Tuesday morning, when I was a brand-new qualified nurse, I drew the short straw and was on the early shift after another very late night at Benny's. At the time we had a student nurse who organised activities for the ward, and to my delight and relief I was told that she'd planned a half-hour relaxation session for the staff at 8.30 a.m.

How lucky am I? I'll be as right as rain after this.

Taking my place on a thin blue gym mat in the large lounge, I closed my eyes as instructed and listened to the tinkling piano music playing on a cassette tape on the portable stereo unit. 'I'd like you all to empty your mind of worries,' a soothing voice said. 'Think only about your breathing, and try to make it as deep and even as you can.'

I didn't hear anything else because I dropped off to sleep, which was hardly surprising after having approximately four hours' sleep the night before. Unfortunately, I must have fallen into a very deep sleep indeed, because when I finally woke up I was shocked to discover it was four o'clock in the afternoon. Not only that, but everybody else had left the lounge and I'd therefore been there all alone for hours on end, the keys to the unit loose in my pocket.

I jumped up like a scalded cat, feeling sick to my stomach about what would happen to me now.

I've had it this time. All that training for nothing! They'll get shot of me for sure.

As I walked sheepishly out of the room, smoothing down my dress, I thought about how I'd have to hand my uniform back, and how my days of answering the phone with a cheery, 'Hello! Staff Nurse Gibson, how can I help?' were surely numbered.

Embarrassingly, when I stepped onto the corridor a huge cheer went up from the staff, as well as from several of the patients who seemed to have formed a welcome committee.

'I'm so sorry,' I said to everyone. 'I really can't believe I've done this.'

'No bother,' someone said. 'As long as you're OK. Have you still got your keys?'

'Must have been some relaxation session,' someone else commented.

'It was quite entertaining,' said another. 'You were snoring and dribbling! Ha ha!'

I was mortified and began apologising over and over again, to anyone and everyone who would listen.

'Does the charge nurse know?' I asked. 'Do you think I should jump before I'm pushed?'

My colleagues let me twist in the wind for what seemed like an age before one of my friends eventually took pity on me and spilled the beans. 'Don't look so scared!' she laughed. 'We've got a confession to make.'

It turned out that the real time was 9 a.m. As soon as I fell asleep – moments into the class, by all accounts – the staff and patients rushed around changing all the clocks on the unit, and all their watches, instead of continuing the session.

'You bastards!' I cried. 'You absolute bastards!'

On another Tuesday morning my friend Jack came in hungover and also extremely short of sleep, not least because he had a new puppy who'd woken up several times in the night. As the unit was quiet he went for a lie-down in the seclusion room, asking me to cover for him if need be.

'No problem,' I said. 'Happy to help you out, Jack.'

Not only had Jack played a part in the clock prank, he had also played another trick on me recently, emerging from the toilets carrying one of those rigid paper containers used in commodes. This one was full to the brim, and to my horror Jack shoved it right under my nose.

'Look at this,' he said, watching me recoil from the faeces swimming in urine.

'Go away, that's disgusting!' I said.

To my horror Jack then grabbed hold of the faeces and put it in his mouth. I felt my stomach do a somersault and put my hand over my mouth and nose.

'Jack! What's wrong with you? Stop it!'

Sally was standing beside me and she instantly turned away and started to gag, shouting at Jack to 'Pack it in, you animal!'

Jack couldn't keep his face straight a moment longer, and through gasps of laughter he told us that we were a ridiculously gullible pair, and did we really think he would do such a thing?

'What is it, then?' I asked. 'Because it looks very real to me.'

Jack milked the situation for as long as he could.

'I'll tell you, when Sally's recovered! How can you be a nurse and be so squeamish?'

Eventually he described how he'd melted a Mars bar in the kitchen, squished it up and floated it in some yellow lemonade.

Needless to say, I'd been looking for a chance to get my revenge on Jack after being pranked by him not once but twice, and when he went for his sleep in the seclusion room I saw a golden opportunity. As soon as I was sure he was snoring away, I snuck in with a jug of water and carefully dribbled it around his crotch, making it look like he'd wet himself. Jack must have been exhausted, because he didn't move a muscle or stir at all.

Half an hour later I returned with a cheerful, 'Jack, you'd better wake up now. It's 9 a.m.'

'Thanks, Belinda,' he said, before looking down between his legs and turning crimson.

'Oh my God, I've never done that before!' he said. 'Shit!'

'I wouldn't worry about it, these things happen,' I said, with a teasing smile. 'Perhaps you should have taken a commode into the seclusion room with you?'

'Very funny!' he said.

I'd given him a hint there, but Jack didn't suspect a thing, instead spending the whole day telling me he was so embarrassed, and he had no idea why that had happened. 'I need to train that puppy to sleep through the night! I can't risk this happening again, bloody hell!'

I fully expected Jack to twig the next day, or the next, or at least have some suspicions, but he never did. Instead he shamefully accepted the fact he'd peed his pants in his sleep, in the seclusion room, and with me as the chief witness. On top of this he volunteered the information to our colleagues, no doubt wanting to have some agency in the story.

It was many years later, when out of the blue somebody poked fun at him for his supposed 'incontinence', that I finally felt it was time to set the record straight. Jack's jaw dropped to his chest when I made my confession, but he was remarkably forgiving. 'I guess I deserved it,' he said. 'Mind you, the irony is I had sleepless nights over that, which was the very last thing I needed!'

'I'm sorry to be the bearer of bad news, but Claudia has taken her own life.'

It was one of the charge nurses, delivering the news in a brisk but not unkind way at the morning handover meeting. 'She hadn't been seen for a few days, but nobody was worried as she appeared to be really well. Her family thought she'd taken herself away somewhere, seeing as she had some time off work.'

As with Gary, I think there was a sense of inevitability that Claudia's life would end this way, but nevertheless it was still a massive shock to my colleagues and me. As was typically the case, the demands of the ward quickly took over and the shift continued, giving us no time to stop and reflect on the loss.

It was some time later, following an inquest into her death, that we learned more details about Claudia's passing. She had spent her last few days getting her affairs in order, including visiting her close friend Astrid to help fix her music stereo, something she had been promising to do for weeks. Claudia had also cleared a lot of junk out of her loft, taking bags of books and clothes to the charity shop, and had visited family members she hadn't seen for a long time. This desire to tie up loose ends is typical behaviour in someone who is preparing to commit suicide, and it is not uncommon for the person to be in surprisingly good spirits, relieved that the end is near and their suffering, or their cycle of suffering, will soon be over.

With her jobs completed, Claudia booked herself into a local hotel, smiling and chatting in a friendly manner with the receptionist before going to her room and putting a 'Do not disturb' sign outside the door. Over a period of several hours, thirty-year-old Claudia proceeded to overdose on painkillers washed down with vodka.

It was a few days before a housekeeper found her, having used a master key to open the hotel-room door after Claudia failed to respond to her repeated knocking. When the room was searched Claudia had apparently left no note – I say apparently because I've known of instances where letters have been removed and destroyed if it was thought that they would only add to the misery of remaining friends and family.

My overwhelming reaction was that it was such a sad waste of a good life. Claudia was a wonderful person, and like many people who knew her well I felt guilty that this had happened. With her long and well-known history of severe depression, I inevitably wondered if I could have done anything to prevent this outcome. In hindsight, Claudia's behaviour in the days and weeks before her death should have made her intentions quite obvious, especially to all the mental health nurses she counted amongst her friends. When she died she was still employed as a staff nurse on Ward 14, and had been at work in the days and weeks before she went missing. Why had nobody spotted the warning signs?

I and many other nurses went to Claudia's funeral, and afterwards we all went to the pub and got drunk. After her inquest, local press and TV reports highlighted the fact she was a qualified staff nurse working on a secure psychiatric ward, a job that was described by the coroner as 'stressful' and 'highly pressurised'. Her history of depression and alcohol dependency was also made public, information the media seemed to think was surprising and unusual given her line of work, the assumption appearing to be that a professional mental health nurse would somehow be immune from the problems that afflicted her patients. How little they knew, I thought, thinking of the many colleagues I knew who had depression and felt suicidal (or had killed themselves), as well as those who medicated themselves with alcohol or were alcohol- or drug-dependent.

I wondered if the outcome for Claudia might have been different if she had worked in a less emotionally demanding job and if her problems were not exacerbated by her reliance on alcohol. We will never know. The majority of my colleagues who were heavy drinkers, binge drinkers and functioning alcoholics managed to progress and maintain a successful nursing career whilst balancing their alcohol intake. Astrid, certainly, had survived this way for years, although I was very sorry to see that after Claudia's death her already extreme drinking habits intensified still further.

One evening I invited Astrid back to our narrowboat, and on the way she picked up a bottle of vodka in the corner shop and drank the whole lot in a few hours, though she barely appeared to be drunk. Astrid had always been a very blunt person, and that evening she told me bitterly that Claudia had promised her she would never take her own life, and that she felt betrayed and abandoned by her friend.

As well as drinking excessively every day, Astrid began taking all kinds of drugs, illegal as well as prescription. Unsurprisingly, she was no longer managing to function as normally at work as she had done before, and it was just eighteen months after Claudia's suicide when Astrid was dismissed from her job and ultimately struck off the nursing register because of her addictions.

Unlike Claudia, Astrid had very few friends and no family living nearby, and she led a very sad and isolated life. Ultimately, losing Claudia had been too much to bear. Two years after her friend's death, forty-one-year-old Astrid caught a train to Skegness, bought an antique sword at a car boot sale and, when she returned to her flat later that day, used it to slash both her wrists.

I knew plenty of other nurses who took drugs, many stealing them from work. The medicine cabinet was a huge old metal chest on wheels that not only had a lock on its doors but always stood in the locked clinic room, usually chained to the wall, near to the locked medicine fridge and shelves full of dressings and sterile tape. Despite having all of these measures in place, back in the day anyone who had the 'meds bunch' could access both the medicine cabinet and fridge. This bunch of keys was passed around freely throughout the shift, fished out of one pocket and shoved into another, meaning any of the staff could access the packets and bottles of medicines that were being used on the ward. As with the stores of cleaning products, there was no inventory nor any budget restraints. The pharmacist would regularly visit the ward and top up whichever tablets were low, just like restocking shelves in a supermarket.

The only drugs that were always accounted for were the controlled drugs like methadone and morphine, which were addictive and could be misused. They were kept in a separate cabinet that had a more substantial lock on it. We still had the keys, but all the controlled drugs had to be counted in and out and signed for by name.

None of the medication (controlled drugs included) was marked up for individual use, and this didn't start to change until the early 1990s. Even then it was a gradual tightening up, and it would be several more years before we reached the standards in place today, whereby each patient has medicine labelled with their name and date of birth and it is counted in and out by two members of staff, just like a prescription ordered from the pharmacy by a GP.

Suffice to say, the medicine chest was ripe for exploitation, and some nurses helped themselves as if it were the pick 'n' mix stand at Woolworths. For example, there was one cheeky male nurse who would brazenly swallow two lorazepam tablets before he left work, though typically only at the end of the month.

'You should try it,' Lenny said to me, tellingly, after hearing me complaining about the interest rate spiralling to more than 12 per cent just as I'd taken out my first mortgage.

'Why?' I replied, giving him a cheeky smile. 'I have no trouble sleeping. In fact, I could sleep on a washing line after a shift in here.'

I was being deliberately obtuse. This nurse's reason for taking the drug – typically used to treat anxiety and sleeping problems – was common knowledge amongst his colleagues, though we all chose to say nothing. The recession was biting and all the staff were looking for ways to save money. The wife of another male nurse, for instance, ran a chain of hairdressers, and he was in the habit of bringing in all the towels from the salons whenever he did a night shift, and brazenly washing and drying them in the hospital laundry. One night the laundry door wouldn't open, which didn't please him one bit, though instead of taking the dirty washing home he decided there was only one thing for it, and proceeded to kick the laundry door in. Before the nurse went home with his piles of clean towels he wrote in the log that one of the patients 'had an unsettled night and forced open the laundry room door by kicking it repeatedly'. Again we all turned a blind eye – who was I to judge?

Meanwhile, Lenny the lorazepam looter had worked out that if he popped a couple of pills before going to the pub, he'd only have to buy two pints to feel drunk, helping him save valuable pounds and eke out his salary until payday!

Finn was another male nurse who raided the medicine cabinet, and he was probably the worst offender of all. Finn loved drugs, and there wasn't one pill or potion in the medicine chest or fridge that he hadn't tried. Diazepam was his favourite – 'Helps me sleep' – and Kemadrin came a close second – 'Gives me a buzz'. Both were in endless supply on the ward, Kemadrin (also known as procyclidine) being commonly used to combat the side effects of some of the older anti-psychotics such as chlorpromazine, notably the jerky, involuntary movements it induces. Mind you, as with many drugs designed to combat the symptoms of other medications, Kemadrin has its own side effects, including drowsiness, blurred vision and nervousness, for which you could take other medication. It was a bit of a vicious circle, to say the least.

Finn was a very solitary character who was always the first to volunteer to 'watch' the TV lounge for the shift, keeping himself (and his habits) to himself and having the bare minimum of interaction with other staff. If you did manage to engage him in conversation he made no secret of the fact he would have preferred to be fishing in the Lake District, which he did as often as he possibly could.

One summer – July 1985 to be precise, as it was when the Live Aid concert was on – Finn failed to return to work after a two-week holiday to Ullswater. I found out afterwards that one of the friendlier charge nurses had had a quiet word with him before he went away. 'You're a nice guy, but not a great nurse,' Finn was told. 'Perhaps it would be a good idea if you considered retraining, trying a different profession?'

Finn apparently took little persuading to leave the hospital, and he disappeared off the radar for many years before I heard his name mentioned again.

'Remember that nurse who used to drop a tab of LSD before he came to work?' Jonathan said one day.

'No, I don't know who you mean,' I replied.

'You must do! Finn, his name was. Really quiet guy, into fishing. He used to nick stuff from the medicine cabinet, and he thought nobody noticed.'

'Oh!' I said. 'I do know who you mean, but I had no idea about the LSD.'

There was another surprise in store, as Jonathan went on to tell me that he'd heard Finn had retrained, as he'd been advised to do all those years before.

'Good for him,' I said, a picture forming in my mind of Finn sailing across a picturesque lake, perhaps giving a guided tour to a group of anglers. 'What as?'

'A doctor,' Jonathan said, cracking up laughing.

I was flabbergasted. 'Are you serious?'

'Absolutely. He's working in A & E at the general hospital.'

Rather like feelings, I guess ambition has to come out somehow, however unlikely and surprising Finn's reincarnation as a doctor was. When it sank in, I hoped he had finally found his true calling. Mental health nursing, and on a locked ward to boot, is certainly not for everyone. I found myself reflecting on how my mother dragged me out of my bed all those years before, adamant that was I was not going to be a 'one in ten', and how lucky I was that I found my vocation.

Throughout my career I've worked with plenty of other nurses like Lenny and Finn who really didn't have their heart in their work. The patients they worked with are better off for people like that leaving the profession. In today's more regulated environment, Lenny and Finn probably wouldn't even get past the starting post, so at least progress has been made in that regard. Other colleagues like Claudia were outstanding nurses, but their own mental health needs left them struggling at times.

That said, the majority I've worked with were (or still are) fantastic mental health nurses, amongst them Jonathan, Neil, Sally,

Nicola, Gayle and Jack. They really wanted to improve the lives of patients and they genuinely cared, and that is what counts. There are legions of compassionate nurses working in mental health, and we are very lucky to have them looking after us and our loved ones.

Epilogue

I arrived at work to see Josephine standing under an umbrella with a group of other elderly patients on the gravel driveway. She seemed her usual cheerful self and was happy to do as she was told, lining up to board the waiting hospital minibus. Beyond her, the hospital's imposing clock tower quivered under a veil of mist and drizzle, the hands of the clock as still and empty as the wards and abandoned outbuildings scattered all around.

It was the early 1990s and Josephine had lived at the hospital for approximately four decades, ever since her admission following the birth of her illegitimate child in the 1950s. Besides a handful of trips to North Wales she'd lived out the majority of her adult life inside the hospital. Today all that would change, and she would be driven out of the rusting iron gates one last time.

I stopped and sheltered under a tree, taking in the scene from beneath the hood of my raincoat. They say that when a person is dying the physical change in their appearance is a way of preparing their loved ones for their departure. I don't know if there's any scientific proof for this, but it's something I've witnessed many times. And in that moment, I realised that was what had been happening to the hospital for months on end, the life gradually being sucked out of it before our eyes.

'Will it be sunnier there?' I heard Josephine ask loudly, a song in her voice as usual. 'Are we going to a cafe on the way?'

'No, love, I don't think so,' a kindly nurse replied with a smile, unable to disguise the sadness in her voice. 'You'll be there in an hour or so, it's not very far.'

With the exception of Josephine, the assembled patients – perhaps a dozen or so – looked as sad and dejected as the hospital itself. Scared and confused, they were full of questions and trepidation about the journey they were about to embark on.

'You'll like it there,' all the nurses were reassuring them. 'You're going back to your home town and you'll have a room of your own. Won't that be nice?'

'But I don't want to go,' said a stooped gentleman with a stick, shaking his head despondently. 'I like it here. Is Harold coming? I want to stay put.'

'Here, have another cig,' a nurse coaxed. 'And let's find you a seat, shall we? Come on, let me help you up the step. I'm sure you're going to love it when you get there. You're going home!'

Ever since the mid-1980s we'd been told that the hospital would be permanently shut down one day, in step with Margaret

Thatcher's plans to introduce the government's new policy of Care in the Community. The modern reforms were a cost-effective way of moving with the times and finally abolishing the crumbling Victorian asylums, we were told. Patients with a mental health diagnosis would receive better care in a home of their own, in supported accommodation or care homes, or in smaller psychiatric units.

None of the staff quite believed our hospital would close, myself included. 'Where will all the patients go?' was the familiar refrain whenever the subject cropped up, as it did sporadically throughout the second half of the 1980s. We had hundreds of patients in our hospital alone, and if all of the UK's vast old psychiatric hospitals were shut down more than 100,000 patients would need to be relocated. 'It'll never happen,' colleagues always concluded. 'How can it?' I found myself agreeing with them, or at least I couldn't quite bring myself to disagree – after all, the hospital was my home too, in many ways.

By the start of the 1990s a date had been set for the closure of the hospital and our period of denial was brought to a shuddering halt. A new hospital manager was swiftly parachuted in to coordinate the closure. He was instantly despised by all, and not long after his arrival a cartoon appeared in the staff newsletter, depicting him as a crazed megalomaniac, cruelly throwing out patients onto the street.

'I will find those responsible!' he scowled, though he never did get to the bottom of it; our lips were sealed.

One by one, over a period of many months, the forty-plus wards gradually started to empty out and shut down, minibuses and coaches arriving regularly to ferry the patients to their new homes and hospital units. Though the cartoon was a gross exaggeration of how this was managed, I did hear stories of patients who had to be dragged out of the door, in some cases kicking and screaming.

The fate of each and every patient in the hospital was decided by doctors and nurses, as well as psychologists, psychiatrists, occupational therapists and other professionals, if it was deemed necessary. Those who were elderly and incapable of living independently after years on long-stay wards were generally moved into newly built care homes or small hospitals, the latter usually located in rough parts of town or built at the back of large general hospitals.

Lena fell into this category, as did the elderly female patients from Sister Kane's old ward, and men like Olek from the male rehabilitation ward. In the main these patients had no relatives or contacts at all in the outside world and were considered to have ongoing care needs that required some form of institutional-style setting. In other words, for those men and women nothing much would change in terms of the treatment and care they were given, they would simply lose the benefits of living in a self-contained community with people they knew, and in the beautiful surroundings they had become accustomed to.

Any patients who had originally been admitted to the hospital 'out of area' – however long ago that was – were returned to their own local authority, which then became responsible for their care. Josephine and her fellow minibus travellers came under this heading, which was why some of the nurses were telling them they were going 'home'. My heart went out to them; most of the frail old people who were being bribed onto the bus with fags probably had precious few memories, if any at all, of the place they once called home. The reality was that they would be starting from scratch in a town they didn't recognise, separated from friends and people they had lived with for years and being looked after by staff who didn't know them from Adam – a very tall (if not impossible) order for an elderly person with mental health needs.

The remaining patients were sent to supported living accommodation or placed in their own flats and houses, with varying levels of support provided at home and/or in the community.

As the patients were driven away to their new lives and their old wards shut down, security staff replaced nurses, men in uniforms patrolling the site and guarding the derelict buildings. The gardeners and maintenance staff were amongst the first to be put out to grass and the grounds became wildly overgrown, ivy growing up the walls and windows of the outbuildings, and the tennis nets turning black with mould and sagging like old bandages. Meanwhile bricks were crumbling, window frames rotting and tiles falling off roofs everywhere you looked. Pint pots gathered cobwebs on the very sorry-looking closed-down bar, and the already faded glory of the ballroom turned completely to dust, the disused dance floor now cracked and creaking like old bones.

Ward 14 was the very last to close, and in its final few weeks and days it stood at the end of a long, dead corridor. Sometimes you don't recognise the end of an era until you look back, but the haemorrhaging of life from the old asylum was conspicuous and palpable, scenes like the one I witnessed with Josephine providing unavoidable reminders. It seemed that every time I arrived for work something else was gone – whole rows of cars in the staff car park, the sound of voices carried down distant corridors and the lights in yet another gutted outbuilding.

There were many occasions when I stopped on my way into work and looked around the shell of the old hospital, my mind wandering back in time. Looking at the windows of the old long-stay wards I saw myself dancing with Olek, and finding myself suddenly falling in love with the job after my shaky start. From that day on I enjoyed coming to work so much that I often left my clapped-out little car at home and took the special 'works' bus from town with the other nursing assistants, because we always had so much fun together. The memory made me smile; I'd had a brilliant time here.

When I embarked on my nurse training my friends bought me my own LP of *The Sound of Music*. 'My Favourite Things' had become my signature tune and I had played it *all* the time, encouraging countless patients – not just Olek – to join me for a dance. The album was the soundtrack to my early years in nursing, and remembering those days filled my heart with joy, stirring memories I would never forget.

Looking across the empty car park I could picture Sally with her head hanging from the door of my Mini, sleeping off her afternoon drinks. Beyond her, walking in the grounds, I could almost hear Aggie and me singing 'True', her arm linked in mine. Other days I remembered Helen and Bernadette, my memory of them as clear as day, laughing their heads off as they stood outside the entrance to the morgue. I thought about dear old Ernie too, letting me lead him across the garden to a dance in the ballroom. He had been one of the very first patients to leave the hospital and had been placed in a specialist care home not far from the town centre. I found out later that he survived for only a short time there, which upset me. He had become bedbound before passing away in his sleep; I loved that man so much and I wished I'd had the chance to say goodbye.

Fortunately for the staff and patients of Ward 14, we were all moving together into a new psychiatric unit on the fringes of town. Our purpose-built hospital was a modern concrete box with a flat roof, situated in a run-down area surrounded by streets of terraced houses and a parade of tatty takeaways. The unit had no grounds around it to speak of, just a sad bit of landscaping around the edges of the building and a large car park at the back containing a bank of rubbish bins. It was sterile and prison-like compared to what we were used to, its modern furniture bolted to the floor with conspicuous shiny fixings, and harsh strip lights illuminating the corridors like flashlights. Outside there were a couple of small grey yards to sit in, encased in high metal fencing. We could sort those out and make them more useful and appealing, I thought.

Our fifteen patients had known the move was imminent for a long time and were remarkably accepting of the situation – in some cases, more so than the staff. Whenever they asked questions we repeated the same hopes and dreams. *It's been built just for us. The building is new and modern. You'll all have your own bedroom. You'll be able to go out more as it's closer to the shops.*

For those used to sleeping in the male and female dormitories as opposed to single bedrooms the move was a much easier sell, and I think the younger patients were generally more willing to accept the change, not least because of the lure of modern fixtures and fittings.

A small percentage of our colleagues chose not to transfer to the new unit, including the little nurse Nicola, who opted to leave nursing altogether, and Sally, who was pregnant and taking a career break. Meanwhile Sister Judy took a better-paid job in the private sector, a move that surprised nobody. She didn't last long, we soon discovered, her incompetence and unsuitability for the job being rapidly exposed. After being demoted down to staff nurse she left the profession with her tail between her legs. I have no idea what she did next – nobody I knew kept in contact with her.

Many of the nurses who worked on the long-stay and other open wards in the hospital also chose to leave nursing, and particularly those close to retirement age. In many cases the hospital had been their only employer and they didn't relish the challenge of starting a new chapter in deinstitutionalised care.

From the day I first heard the term, 'Care in the Community',

I had mixed feelings about how it would work. In theory, who could argue with a policy that would encourage the care of some of the most vulnerable members of society in their own homes, or at least in more personalised settings than a vast asylum? In practice, however, a person with a mental health diagnosis needs a very strong network around them of paid and unpaid support, especially when they have complex needs alongside their mental health problems. How would that work for patients who had no family and whose only friends had been inside the old hospital?

When the transfer of patients from Ward 14 began, staff were divided between the old hospital and the new unit as we gradually made the move over a few days. It was chaotic as we packed up the patients' clothes, personal belongings, medical records and so on, but that was no bad thing. When our long-term patients like Agatha, Benedict, Rex and Seth left the ward, everything was so hectic it happened almost without me noticing. There was certainly no time to stand and reflect on how long this had been their home, and what a big step it was to leave. The door simply locked behind them one last time, and off they went, looking forward, not back.

Nikolajs was the very last patient I escorted out of the ward. All the other nurses had left and we were practically the last two souls to leave the echoing hospital.

'How are you?' I asked as we walked arm in arm towards the waiting bus.

'Goo,' Nikolajs said, stopping to take hold of my hand and kiss it before climbing aboard. 'How are you, Be-lin-da?'

'Very good, thank you,' I said, and I was. You have to move with the times, and I was prepared to stay positive and hope for the best.

As the bus snaked down the long driveway I looked back over my shoulder and caught a final glimpse of the old hospital as it disappeared from view. *Bye-bye, and thank you for everything.*

To my surprise, I saw a young nurse standing in front of the main entrance, her head held high and a broad smile on her face. She was very young and a bit cheeky-looking, and she was dressed in a shapeless sack-brown uniform, American-tan tights and sensible flat black brogues.

I smiled back. She had done herself proud, and I gave her a little wave as she faded away.

Enoch Powell was the first politician to promise a new model of care for mental health patients, giving a visionary speech in 1961 in which he pledged to tear down the old asylums. It was an era when large-scale psychiatric hospitals like ours were still operated like prisons regardless of the risk a patient posed, abuse was endemic and patients had little or no say over their treatment. Far from being a place of refuge, asylums had come to be viewed by the public as industrial-sized human dumping grounds.

When Care in the Community finally started to be talked about and introduced more than two decades later, it was championed as a long-awaited antidote to a system of care long past its sell-by date. Patients would no longer be the passive recipients of psychiatric care. Instead they would be empowered to challenge their doctors and live a more independent life, and the abuses of the past would, it was hoped, die with the asylums.

The Care in the Community dream was over very quickly. In December 1992 – even before the phased implementation of most of the changes came into effect in April 1993 – Christopher Clunis killed Jonathan Zito by stabbing him in the eye at Finsbury Park tube station in London. It was a random, unprovoked attack; Christopher had paranoid schizophrenia and had been recently discharged from hospital in line with the Community Care Act of 1990. The case led to the Clunis Report, which cited an extensive catalogue of failures in the care and support of Christopher from all agencies. The tragedy became the most notorious of many violent acts carried out by people with a mental health diagnosis. It not only shocked and panicked the public, but it called the future of Care in the Community into question.

In 1994 the Royal College of Psychiatrists published figures* showing that in the previous three years thirty-four people had killed someone within a year of being in contact with psychiatric services. At the time there were 750,000 patients covered by the Care in the Community scheme, though that was not the figure that attracted attention.

A few years later a BBC *Panorama* documentary filmed police officers being briefed by a psychiatrist about a patient who was making threats to kill. Shocking footage broadcast in 1997 showed

---

* http://news.bbc.co.uk/1/hi/health/218381.stm

a group of police officers forcefully smashing their way into the patient's home – another unwelcome insight into psychiatric services under Care in the Community. By now the public equated the policy with uncontrolled, mentally ill people causing mayhem in society, threatening their safety and their lives.

In 1998 the newly elected Labour Health Secretary Frank Dobson declared Care in the Community a failure and pledged to scrap it, though ultimately the political response was to bring in restrictive legislation. This gave doctors powers to force patients in the community to take their medication or risk losing their newfound freedom – a backwards step, in the eyes of many. Broadly speaking, this is where we still stand – and young black men, incidentally, have a higher rate of forced treatment in the community than any other group.

From where I was standing, on the front line of change, Care in the Community impacted me and my patients in many ways. I had worked with the same core group of staff for years, but now nurses started to come and go at the new unit frequently, and the ratio of unqualified nursing assistants increased as budgets began to bite. I noticed that the strong, unspoken sense of camaraderie I always felt at the old hospital declined; the instinctive way old friends and colleagues looked out for one another simply wasn't there any more.

The unregulated days of staff helping themselves to drugs from the medicine chest, sleeping on the job, drinking lager on duty and massaging the truth in the daily log became a thing of the past as rules and regulations tightened. In short, we had to become a lot more professional or risk being disciplined or struck off. By and large this was a good thing, although it meant a lot of the fun had gone.

Security was tighter than at the old hospital. Instead of having one locked door onto Ward 14, we now had a system of airlocks between entrance and exit doors. Our personal alarms and keys had to be strapped to us at all times, with no exception, and as well as having high fences all around the unit there were huge restrictors on the windows which meant they would hardly open. These heightened security measures were necessary, as we started to admit more patients from prison for assessment, though our patients didn't appreciate the prison-like look and feel of the unit at all, especially those used to living on the comparatively homely Ward 14. Some complained that they felt like inmates, not patients – a word that was widely used in Victorian asylums.

In time we tried to make one of the yards more appealing, putting in a polytunnel, sheds and a greenhouse and growing our own veg, and we acquired a couple of bikes and took some of the patients out for rides when possible. It was *something*, but we could never recreate the grand, self-contained community we enjoyed at the old hospital.

Only one thing remained constant. The treatment the patients received was largely the same – it was simply provided in a smaller and less congenial setting. In other words, for our patients Care in the Community had added next to nothing and taken quite a lot away.

Agatha settled into the rhythm of the new place quite easily, helped in no small way by the fact she was allowed to spend her allowance on ordered-in takeaways instead of having to eat the hospital food every day. Her mental state remained stable, and after a couple of years she was moved to a private secure unit in another part of the country. I missed her a great deal, but it was the right move for Aggie – her new unit was far less prison-like than ours, with some on-site facilities to occupy her, and I hear she continues to do well. Even now, so many years later, I often think of her, and any Spandau Ballet song always makes me smile.

Seth never changed, grumbling every day, being outrageously rude and sexist and getting himself into increasingly hot water with the young nurses. It's safe to say the arrival of the Spice Girls and Girl Power did him no favours whatsoever. Seth lived at the unit for about a year and a half before being transferred to a specialist nursing home for people with severe mental health diagnoses and low levels of risk. Nikolajs joined him soon afterwards, though you would never have known the two men had spent more than a decade sitting side by side in the old hospital. By all accounts they never went near each other, let alone communicated. Seth rarely left the building and passed away just a couple of years later, while Nikolajs enjoyed many more years, during which time he learned to cook and loved doing jigsaws. He passed away at a ripe old age, after having a fall and contracting pneumonia in hospital.

Of all the Ward 14 patients, Benedict took the longest time to settle into the new unit. I continued to cajole him to wash with a forthright but cheeky, 'You smell!', though it was harder now as we had mostly showers instead of the big old Victorian bathtubs he was used to soaking in. Benedict's addiction to nicotine and sugar never abated and he died young, in his sixties, a few years after being transferred to a care home.

Figures show* people living with severe mental health diagnoses die fifteen to twenty years earlier than the general population, largely due to preventable or treatable physical health problems. I've seen many patients like Benedict with paranoid schizophrenia and other severe mental health conditions die prematurely as a result of the strong drugs they take and their lifestyle choices. Jay, sadly, was another example. I had not seen him for years and he never came to the new unit, though I knew he was still a 'revolving door' patient, being admitted time and again onto various other psychiatric units in the area after repeated paranoid and psychotic episodes (some involving samurai swords and altercations with the police, others not). Very sadly, Jay was diagnosed with cancer while still in his thirties, and he died soon afterwards, having refused treatment.

Our pub singer Victor has also passed away, very recently in fact. I heard he had been put on some new medication and became constipated in his supported living flat. As nobody was monitoring him and he didn't know it was important to tell anyone, he tragically died of poisoning.

---

* https://www.england.nhs.uk/statistics/wp-content/uploads/sites/2/2019/08/Physical-Health-Checks-SMI-Statistical-Press-Notice-2019-20-Q1.pdf

In 2016, the Five Year Forward View for Mental Health (FYFVMH) set out NHS England's approach to reducing the stark levels of premature mortality for people living with severe mental illness, who die fifteen to twenty years earlier than the general population, largely due to preventable or treatable physical health problems.

As for Rex, he stayed with us in the new unit for about two years. When he lost his strength (and hence the ability to be physically violent) he was moved into an unlocked unit and eventually a care home, where he still resides. I discovered very recently that Rex eventually lost his hatred of 'fucking Jonathan Black'. Jonathan knows the care home well and recognised Rex's description from a colleague; he is still a large, squat man with a voice like Barry White, though forty years on his wiry black beard is as white as snow. Jonathan paid him a visit last year. 'My man!' Rex said immediately. 'It's so good to see you!' Rex is in his seventies now, doing really well, and is still in close contact with the surviving members of his family.

Of all the original Ward 14 patients, Stuart stayed the longest on the new unit, living there for almost four years. His mum Gladys drowned herself in the canal after many mental health crises, and not long after her death Stuart was reassessed and transferred to a private secure unit. I left shortly after Stuart. Jonathan and I were ready to start a family, so it was time for new beginnings for me too.

I couldn't wait to be a mum and was full of hope when I underwent IVF treatment, but by 2000 Jonathan and I had to face the fact that it had failed and we needed to move on. We decided to volunteer to work in Africa, taking a year-long sabbatical from the NHS before looking into adoption. By this time I'd worked at two other secure units and as a court liaison officer, working out of a custody suite in a busy police station. However, nothing could have prepared me for Africa.

Through a charity, Jonathan and I were posted to a psychiatric hospital in Zambia, a place where patients with epilepsy were still being incarcerated, and were considered to be possessed by the Devil. The hospital had no psychiatrist and there was never enough anti-psychotic medication to go around, so it was left to nurses like us to give what few drugs we had to whoever we thought was in the greatest need. People came from all over Zambia, often walking miles, and every day I was taking away more than I contributed, being educated endlessly about the limitless need for kindness and sensitivity, and learning more than I ever knew about the importance of not judging others until you knew their full story.

It was the height of the AIDS epidemic and a whole generation of Zambians had been wiped out. Jonathan decided to change jobs and went to work at the Fountain of Hope, a centre that provided medical care, food and a place to sleep for orphaned children who had nowhere to go. The premises consisted of a dusty piece of land surrounded by a concrete wall and a couple of miserable buildings where the children slept on the floor, and Jonathan worked out of a boiling-hot metal shipping container, consulting the handbook, *Where There is No Doctor* by David Werner, when he needed help. Many of the children had lost their parents to AIDS – or 'slims disease' as the locals called it, due to the amount of weight people lost prior to death.

One day, just before Jonathan had a weekend off, a small boy wandered into the centre. He was quite ill and needed some antibiotics, but over the weekend there were no staff to care for him. We lived in a shack where I used to sit and cry at night under the mosquito nets, thinking about all of our patients and how they suffered. The shack was running with cockroaches but it was far more comfortable than the conditions the children endured at the centre, and Jonathan brought the little boy home so he could make sure he took his antibiotics and give him the care he needed. The boy was very sweet and managed to tell us his name was Gypsy, and by the end of the weekend I was so sad to see him leave.

When they returned to the centre, Gypsy sat by Jonathan's Land Rover all day long, and as Jonathan climbed into the car at the end of the day he looked down to see a tear rolling down Gypsy's little face. One tear, but it changed all of our lives, forever. Jonathan leant down, picked the boy up and put him in the car. I was sat watching TV when they arrived home, and I looked up to see a beautiful, smiley face peeping out from behind Jonathan's legs. It was our little Gypsy Boy, and that was that – he was ours. It's strange, but looking back we feel that he was always ours, he was destined to be ours. We were all just waiting to find each other.

The charity we were working with was *very* unhappy about Gypsy and our plans to adopt him, and they refused to put him on our health insurance until we caused a huge fuss and they relented. Reams of red tape later, we left Africa earlier than planned after discovering Gypsy had an enlarged heart and there was no treatment in Zambia. When we arrived back in the UK the condition had disappeared; we learned that Gypsy had been so malnourished that his heart, as a muscle, had gone floppy.

Once we settled back in England I returned to the small psychiatric unit I worked at after leaving the asylum, but I hated leaving Gypsy and just wanted to be at home with him. A year later, Jonathan, Gypsy and I went to live in a tiny whitewashed mountain village in southern Spain. I wanted to give Gypsy the best childhood and we stayed there for three years, until we ran out of money and had to return to the UK to find work. I went back into secure care in the private sector as a clinical manager, and Jonathan returned to work as a mental health staff nurse.

Today, Gypsy is grown up and has his own little daughter, Penelope, with his lovely wife-to-be Charlotte.

We could not be more proud of him.

It's now thirty years on from the introduction of Care in the Community and I've been asked many times, 'Was it worth it? Has it worked?'

The phrase, 'Throwing the baby out with the bathwater,' comes to mind when I reflect on the closure of the old psychiatric hospital. Yes, there is a strong recovery focus now that did not exist in the early years of my career. Yes, for some people hospitalisation is not beneficial and they are better off being cared for in the community, as long as that care is adequate. But there are always the vulnerable within our society, those who have no support around them, no friends or family, and who have chronic and enduring severe mental ill-health. These people are more suited to living together in a community, where they are cared for with dignity and compassion.

Deinstitutionalisation seemed like a step forward, but in practice cutting costs has come before investment in the proper services required to care for people with mental health diagnoses outside the hospital setting. We now know that for many patients, the seismic change that Care in the Community brought was detrimental to their health and well-being, and it led to an increase in the number of people with mental illness living on the streets and being put in prison.

A return to the asylum system is not the answer, but I would like to see some long-term service provision for those people with severe mental health diagnoses who simply cannot live independently. If money were no object I would like a village created with small houses around a central area of shops, a swimming pool, other leisure services and a small farm, where people could live and work according to their ability, all in a picturesque setting. Most important of all, the nurses would have genuine concern for the well-being of the patients. They would champion their needs and never take no for an answer when planning the best care. Because above all else, compassion must be front and centre of mental health nursing. Without it, you cannot give the patients the care they deserve – and they deserve the very best.

When I retired, as I've said, I refused to give up my registration because to this day I remain fiercely proud to call myself a mental health nurse. I was given so many thoughtful presents from patients and colleagues when I left my last nursing post, but the best gift I will ever have is the knowledge that I *did* do my best for my patients. And that is because I genuinely cared, for each and every one of them.

Acknowledgements

It is hard to know where to start as there have been so many people who have helped me in writing this book, in my life and in my nursing career. But here goes.

Firstly, I would like to thank all the patients I have ever nursed. You taught me care and compassion, which made me the person I am today. Secondly, all the mental health nurses I have known and those to come who are committed to delivering the best care they can for their patients.

Thirdly, Benny's nightclub, Holsten Pils and Southern Comfort!

I would also like to thank literary agent Jonathan Conway, who was interested enough to reply to a random email from someone completely unknown to him and who had never written a book! Thank you, Jonathan, for your belief in me and the project.

I would like to thank my co-writer, the spectacular Rachel Murphy, who not only made this book into a reality but did so with care, compassion and total respect for the stories within it.

I would like to thank all at Quercus for their faith in and passion for this project, and a special mention to Katy Follain.

I would like to thank my favourite son Gypsy William Black just for being his lovely supportive self, and his lovely wife-to-be Ms Charlotte Gosling. My favourite granddaughter Penelope, unbeknown to her, helped me through some recent dark times.

My older sister Joanne (keep going) and my younger sister Tammi – we don't need words. My mother and father, no longer with me, for their constant belief and support as I grew up. 'You can do anything you want,' was a familiar cry from both of them.

Lastly, my husband Jonathan, who has always been there for me no matter what and always believes in me. The wind beneath my wings.